1st EDITION

Perspectives on Diseases and Disorders

Down Syndrome

Dawn Laney

Book Editor

GALE
CENGAGE Learning™

Detroit • New York • San Francisco • New Haven, Conn • Waterville, Maine • London

Christine Nasso, *Publisher*
Elizabeth Des Chenes, *Managing Editor*

© 2008 Greenhaven Press, a part of Gale, Cengage Learning

Gale and Greenhaven Press are registered trademarks used herein under license.

For more information, contact:
Greenhaven Press
27500 Drake Rd.
Farmington Hills, MI 48331-3535
Or you can visit our Internet site at http://gale.cengage.com

Articles in Greenhaven Press anthologies are often edited for length to meet page requirements. In addition, original titles of these works are changed to clearly present the main thesis and to explicitly indicate the author's opinion. Every effort is made to ensure that Greenhaven Press accurately reflects the original intent of the authors. Every effort has been made to trace the owners of copyrighted material.

Cover image copyright Carlos E. Santa Maria, 2008. Used under license from Shutterstock.com.

ISBN: 978-0-7377-4025-7

Library of Congress Control Number: 2008923809

Printed in the United States of America
2 3 4 5 6 7 12 11 10 09 08

CONTENTS

INTRODUCTION

Standard medical reference sources such as *Merriam-Webster's Medical Dictionary* define Down syndrome as "a congenital condition characterized by moderate to severe mental retardation, slanting eyes, a broad short skull, broad hands with short fingers, and by trisomy of the human chromosome numbered 21." While technically true, this definition of Down syndrome does not provide any perspective on the day-to-day life of an individual with Down syndrome, nor does it help most families learn more about the condition. For families facing the difficult decisions related to the well-being of Down syndrome children, both born and unborn, nothing can substitute for hearing real experiences from families living with Down syndrome.

In a 2005 ABC News story, Beth Allard discussed her son's prenatal diagnosis of Down syndrome and her attempts to obtain a fuller definition of the disorder. During Allard's pregnancy her doctor found abnormalities on a routine ultrasound scan that indicated the fetus had an increased risk for Down syndrome. Further prenatal testing confirmed that the baby had Down syndrome. Immediately, Allard was faced with the difficult decision of whether to continue or terminate her pregnancy. As Allard reports in the story, during this time she felt that the doctors "were very negative throughout the whole thing and [I was] told that the child wouldn't be able to read, write or live any sort of productive life." After much soul-searching and discussions with her family, Allard continued her pregnancy and gave birth to her son, Ben. Allard now is involved in the National Down Syndrome Congress and is committed to helping other parents by providing a broader context in which to understand Down syndrome and its impact on a family.

According to a 2005 survey of mothers of children with Down syndrome by Brian Skotko, Allard's experience is not considered unusual. Although some medical professionals do provide a balanced view of Down syndrome, the survey found that physicians often provide a limited picture of modern opportunities for people with the condition. As Skotko states in a 2005 ABC News report, "My prenatal study says that mothers feel they are getting an inaccurate picture of Down syndrome, often without the most current information and balanced description of the possibilities and realities. This, of course, is coming at a critical time when many mothers are deciding whether or not to continue with their pregnancies." Although it has not been studied, Skotko and others suggest that the high rate of termination following a prenatal diagnosis of Down syndrome, about 90 percent in a 1999 survey, is related to the skewed information provided to parents by health professionals.

The need for balanced information has become even more pronounced since January 2, 2007, when the American College of Obstetricians and Gynecologists (ACOG) released new guidelines that recommended screening and diagnostic testing for Down syndrome and other chromosomal abnormalities be offered to all pregnant women regardless of age. In response, more families of individuals with Down syndrome, Down syndrome organizations, and individuals with Down syndrome themselves have embarked on a mission to provide the family perspective to individuals faced with a diagnosis of Down syndrome in their unborn children. The groups ask that physicians and other medical professionals discussing Down syndrome refer individuals with a prenatal diagnosis of the condition to parents and children who have day-to-day experience with the condition. Like Allard, many parents become involved in support groups

and welcome the opportunity to talk to other parents going through the same difficult decision of whether to terminate or continue a pregnancy with the possibility of Down syndrome. For Allard, the decision to continue her pregnancy with Ben was the right one for her and her family, but she says she does not judge parents who may opt to terminate a pregnancy. Allard believes that parents must have adequate information to make the decision that is right for them and should be made aware of the available support networks if they choose to continue their pregnancy.

Understanding the family's role in Down syndrome is essential, as families have driven the change in the public perception of Down syndrome. The past fifty years

Carrie and Chris Arganbright stand in the nursery they've prepared in their Kansas City home. The baby they are expecting has been diagnosed with Down syndrome. The experiences of families living with Down syndrome can be a great help to couples like the Arganbrights. (AP Images)

have resulted in an ideological shift related to the abilities of individuals with Down syndrome. A baby born in the 1950s with Down syndrome would have been expected to live only into his or her teens, would live in an institution, and receive little or no education and health care. Parents were made to feel ashamed of their children and were advised that the best course of action would be to put their children in an institution and forget them. In contrast, a baby with Down syndrome born in 2007 typically lives with his or her parents, has an average life expectancy of sixty years, attends a mainstream school,

A baby girl with Down syndrome. Down syndrome is caused by a genetic defect in chromosome 21. (Lauren Shear/Photo Researchers, Inc.)

and has a good chance of getting a job and living a full, semi-independent adult life. These significant changes occurred in large part as a result of parent advocacy: Parents knew that their children could positively contribute to society and lead a full life, so they lobbied for access to education, medical care, and community resources.

With the advent of new medical technologies, families of Down syndrome individuals are again reaching out to the community at large. This time, the children they lobby for are not their own, but they nevertheless feel compassion and a sense of kinship with families facing difficult decisions and an uncertain future. The Down syndrome community currently works together to ensure that expectant parents are not unduly influenced to undergo prenatal testing or to terminate a pregnancy after receiving a prenatal diagnosis of Down syndrome. The goal is not to condemn individuals who choose not to have a baby with Down syndrome after prenatal diagnosis; rather, the objective is to ensure that families make an educated decision that includes the family experience as well as the medical reality. At the core, the support groups seek to affirm a vision of a diverse and inclusive society in which human rights are respected and differences are celebrated.

CHAPTER 1

Understanding Down Syndrome

Defining Down Syndrome

Rosalyn S. Carson-DeWitt and Bryan R. Cobb

In this selection authors Rosalyn S. Carson-DeWitt and Bryan R. Cobb provide a brief overview of Down syndrome. The viewpoint begins with a review of the symptoms of Down syndrome, including physical features, congenital malformations, developmental delays, and other medical issues. Next, the authors discuss treatment options and the variable prognoses of individuals affected by Down syndrome. Lastly, the selection addresses the diagnosis of Down syndrome. Carson-DeWitt has written and edited hundreds of medical articles for print, Internet, and CD-ROM products. She is the editor in chief of both the *Encyclopedia of Drugs, Alcohol, and Addictive Behavior*, 2nd ed., and *Drugs, Alcohol, and Tobacco: Learning About Drugs, Alcohol, and Addictive Behavior*, both published by Macmillan Reference USA. Cobb has written several medical articles for print and Internet and is the principal applications scientist at Roche Diagnostics Corporation.

Photo on facing page. A child with Down syndome in the play area of a center for Down syndrome in Kuala Lumpur, Malaysia. It is estimated that one child in 660 has Down syndrome worldwide. (Jimin Lai/AFP/AP Images)

Down syndrome is the most common cause of mental retardation. . . .

[Down syndrome] is usually identified at birth through observation of a set of common physical characteristics. Babies with Down syndrome tend to be overly quiet, less responsive, with weak, floppy muscles. Furthermore, a number of physical signs may be present. These include:

- Flat appearing face
- Small head
- Flat bridge of the nose
- Smaller than normal, low-set nose
- Small mouth, with a protruding tongue
- Upward slanting eyes
- Extra folds of skin located at the inside corner of each eye, near the nose (called epicanthal folds)
- Small, outwardly rotated ears
- Small, wide hands
- An unusual, deep crease across the center of the palm (called a simian crease)
- A malformed fifth finger
- A wide space between the big and the second toes
- Unusual creases on the soles of the feet
- Shorter than normal height.

Other types of defects often accompany Down syndrome. About one third of all children with Down syndrome have heart defects. These heart defects are characteristic of Down syndrome, including abnormal openings (or holes) in the walls which separate the heart's chambers (atrial septal defect, ventricular septal defect). These defects result in abnormal patterns of blood flow within the heart, resulting in inefficient oxygen delivery.

Malformations of the gastrointestinal tract are present in about 5–7% of children with Down syndrome. The most common malformation is a narrowed, obstructed duodenum (the part of the intestine into which the stomach empties). This disorder, called duodenal atresia, interferes with the baby's milk or formula leaving the stomach and entering the intestine for digestion. The baby often vomits forcibly after feeding, and cannot gain weight appropriately until the defect is surgically repaired.

Other medical conditions occurring in patients with Down syndrome include an increased chance of developing infections, especially ear infections and pneumonia; certain kidney disorders; thyroid disease; hearing loss; vision impairment requiring glasses (corrective lenses); and a 15-fold increased risk for developing leukemia.

Developmental milestones in a child with Down syndrome are delayed. Due to weak, floppy muscles (hypotonia), babies learn to sit up, crawl, and walk much later than their normal peers. Talking is also delayed. The extent of delayed brain development is considered to be mild-to-moderate. Most people with Down syndrome can learn to perform regular tasks and can have relatively easy jobs (with supervision).

> **FAST FACT**
>
> Ninety-five percent of persons with Down syndrome function in the mild-to-moderate range of mental retardation.

As people with Down syndrome age, they face an increased risk of developing Alzheimer's disease, a degenerative disease that affects the brain. This occurs several decades earlier than the risk of developing Alzheimer's disease in the general population. As people with Down syndrome age, they also have an increased chance of developing a number of other illnesses, including cataracts, thyroid problems, diabetes, leukemia, and seizure disorders.

Treatment

There is no cure for Down syndrome. However, some of the clinical manifestations can be treated. For example, heart defects and duodenal atresia can often be corrected with surgical repair. It was common only a few decades ago to enforce involuntary sterilization of individuals with Down syndrome. Additionally, it used to be common for these patients to be institutionalized. Today, involuntary sterilizations are illegal and most patients reside with their families. Many community support groups exist to help families deal with the emotional effects and to help plan for the affected individuals' future. In general, Down syndrome people tend to be easygoing and good natured.

Prognosis

The prognosis in Down syndrome is variable, depending on the types of complications (heart defects, susceptibility to infections, leukemia) of each affected individual. The severity of the developmental delay also varies. Without the presence of heart defects, about 90% of children with Down syndrome survive past their teenage years. In fact, people with Down syndrome can live until they are 50 years old.

The prognosis for a baby born with Down syndrome has improved compared to previous years. Modern medical treatments, including antibiotics to treat infections, and surgery to treat heart defects and duodenal atresia has greatly increased their life expectancy.

Diagnosis and Prevention

Down syndrome can be diagnosed at birth, when the characteristic physical signs of Down syndrome are noted and chromosome analysis can also be performed to confirm the diagnosis and determine the recurrence risks.

At-risk pregnancies are referred for genetic counseling and prenatal diagnosis. Screening tests are available during a pregnancy to determine if the fetus has Down syndrome. During 14–17 weeks of pregnancy, a substance called AFP (alpha-fetoprotein) can be measured. AFP is normally found circulating in a pregnant woman's blood, but may be unusually high or low with certain disorders. Carrying a baby with Down syndrome

Diagnostic Tests for Down Syndrome

Amniocentesis

- The removal and analysis of a sample of fetal cells from the amniotic fluid.
- Cannot be done until the 14th–18th week of pregnancy.
- Lower risk of miscarriage than chorionic villus sampling.

Chorionic Villus Sampling (CVS)

- Extraction of a tiny amount of fetal tissue at 9 to 11 weeks of pregnancy.
- The tissue is tested for the presence of extra material from chromosome 21.
- Carries a 1–2 percent risk of miscarriage.

Percutaneous Umbilical Blood Sampling (PUBS)

- Most accurate method used to confirm the results of CVS or amniocentesis.
- The tissue is tested for the presence of extra material from chromosome 21.
- PUBS cannot be done until the 18th–22nd week.
- Carries the greatest risk of miscarriage.

Taken from: National Institutes of Health, National Institute of Child Health and Human Development, "Facts About Down Syndrome," August 18, 2006.

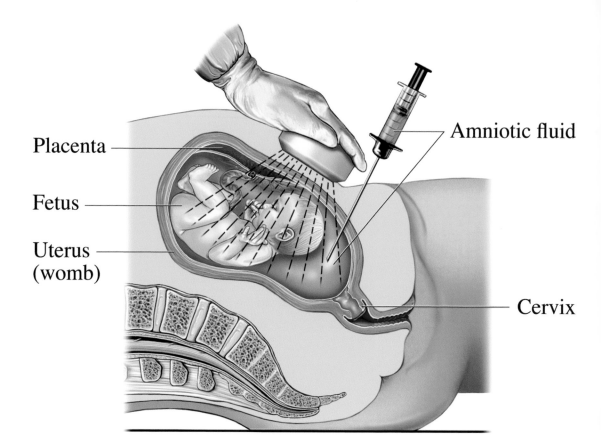

Placenta

Fetus

Uterus (womb)

Amniotic fluid

Cervix

Illustration of an amniocentesis test. A small amount of amniotic fluid is drawn from the uterus with a needle. An amniocentesis can determine with certainly whether a fetus has Down syndrome. (Nucleus Medical Art, Inc./Getty Images)

often causes AFP to be lower than normal. This information alone, or along with measurements of two other hormones, is considered along with the mother's age to calculate the risk of the baby being born with Down syndrome.

A common method to directly determine whether the fetus has Down syndrome, is to test tissue from the fetus. This is usually done either by amniocentesis, or chorionic villus sampling (CVS). In amniocentesis, a small amount of the fluid in which the baby is floating is withdrawn with a long, thin needle. In chorionic villus sampling, a tiny tube is inserted into the opening of the uterus to retrieve a small sample of the chorionic villus (tissue that surrounds the growing fetus). Chromosome analysis follow both amniocentesis and CVS to determine whether the fetus is affected.

Once a couple has had one baby with Down syndrome, they are often concerned about the likelihood of future offspring also being born with the disorder. In most cases, it is unlikely that the risk is greater than other women at a similar age. However, when the baby with Down syndrome has the type that results from a translocation [of genetic material from chromosome 21], it is possible that one of the two parents is a carrier of that defect. When one parent is a carrier of a particular type of translocation, the chance of future offspring having Down syndrome is increased. The specific risks can be estimated by a genetic counselor.

Causes of Down Syndrome

National Institute of Child Health and Human Development

In this information presented by the National Institute of Child Health and Human Development (NICHD), the incidence, cause, and risk of Down syndrome are discussed. Down syndrome is not caused by anything parents did before, during, or after a baby is born. Down syndrome is caused by the addition of extra genetic material from chromosome 21 in the cells of the body. The NICHD, established by Congress in 1962, conducts and supports research on topics related to the health of children, adults, families, and populations.

Named after John Langdon Down, the first physician to identify the syndrome, Down syndrome is the most frequent genetic cause of mild to moderate mental retardation and associated medical problems and occurs in one out of 800 live births, in all

SOURCE: National Institute of Child Health and Human Development, "Facts About Down Syndrome," National Institutes of Health. www.nichd.nih.gov.

races and economic groups. Down syndrome is a chromosomal disorder caused by an error in cell division that results in the presence of an additional third chromosome 21 or "trisomy 21."

The Chromosomal Basis of Down Syndrome

To understand why Down syndrome occurs, the structure and function of the human chromosome must be understood. The human body is made of cells; all cells contain chromosomes, structures that transmit genetic information. Most cells of the human body contain 23 pairs of chromosomes, half of which are inherited from each parent. Only the human reproductive cells, the sperm cells in males and the ovum in females, have 23 *individual* chromosomes, not pairs. Scientists identify these chromosome pairs as the XX pair, present in females, and the XY pair, present in males, and number them 1 through 22.

When the reproductive cells, the sperm and ovum, combine at fertilization, the fertilized egg that results contains 23 chromosome pairs. A fertilized egg that will develop into a female contains chromosome pairs 1 through 22, and the XX pair. A fertilized egg that will develop into a male contains chromosome pairs 1 through 22, and the XY pair. When the fertilized egg contains extra material from chromosome number 21, this results in Down syndrome.

The Genetic Variations That Can Cause Down Syndrome

Three genetic variations can cause Down syndrome. In most cases, approximately 92% of the time, Down syndrome is caused by the presence of an extra chromosome 21 in all cells of the individual. In such cases, the extra chromosome originates in the development of either the egg or the sperm. Consequently, when the egg and sperm unite to form the fertilized egg, three—rather than two—chromosomes 21 are present. As the embryo develops, the extra chromosome is repeated in every cell. This condition, in which three copies of chromosome 21 are present in all cells of the individual, is called trisomy 21.

In approximately 2–4% of cases, Down syndrome is due to mosaic trisomy 21. This situation is similar to simple trisomy 21, but, in this instance, the extra chromosome 21 is present in some, but not all, cells of the individual. For example, the fertilized egg may have the right number of chromosomes, but, due to an error in chromosome division early in embryonic development, some cells acquire an extra chromosome 21. Thus, an individual with Down syndrome due to mosaic trisomy 21 will typically have 46 chromosomes in some cells, but

A karyotype, or picture of chromosomes, showing Down syndrome trisonomy 21. (Phototake Inc./Alamy)

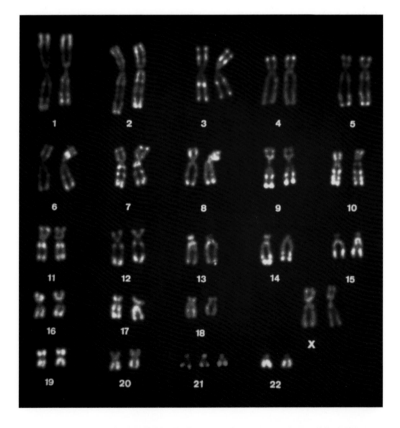

will have 47 chromosomes (including an extra chromosome 21) in others. In this situation, the range of the physical problems may vary, depending on the proportion of cells that carry the additional chromosome 21.

In trisomy 21 and mosaic trisomy 21, Down syndrome occurs because some or all of the cells have 47 chromosomes, including three chromosomes 21. However, approximately 3–4% of individuals with Down syndrome have cells containing 46 chromosomes, but still have the features associated with Down syndrome. How can this be? In such cases, material from one chromosome 21 gets stuck or translocated onto another chromosome, either prior to or at conception. In such situations, cells from individuals with Down syndrome have two normal chromosomes 21, but also have additional chromosome 21 material on the translocated chromosome. Thus, there is still too much material from chromosome 21, resulting in the features associated with Down syndrome. In such situations, the individual with Down syndrome is said to have translocation trisomy 21.

FAST FACT

About five thousand babies with Down syndrome are born in the United States every year.

The Occurrence of Down Syndrome

Most of the time, the occurrence of Down syndrome is due to a random event that occurred during formation of the reproductive cells, the ovum or sperm. As far as we know, Down syndrome is not attributable to any behavioral activity of the parents or environmental factors. The probability that another child with Down syndrome will be born in a subsequent pregnancy is about 1 percent, regardless of maternal age.

For parents of a child with Down syndrome due to translocation trisomy 21, there may be an increased likelihood of Down syndrome in future pregnancies. This is because one of the two parents may be a balanced

The Presence of One Extra Chromosome 21 Results in Down Syndrome

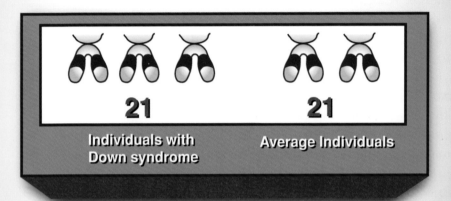

Individuals with Down syndrome

Average Individuals

Taken from: Plano Independent School District, "Trisomy 21 Down Syndrome Chromosomal Disorder," Genetic Disorders Internet & PowerPoint Project, 2000.

carrier of the translocation. The translocation occurs when a piece of chromosome 21 becomes attached to another chromosome, often number 14, during cell division. If the resulting sperm or ovum receives a chromosome 14 (or another chromosome), with a piece of chromosome 21 attached and retains the chromosome 21 that lost a section due to translocation, then the reproductive cells contain the normal or balanced amount of chromosome 21. While there will be no Down syndrome–associated characteristics exhibited, the individual who develops from this fertilized egg will be a carrier of Down syndrome. Genetic counseling can be sought to find the origin of the translocation.

However, it is important to realize that not all parents of individuals with translocation trisomy 21 are themselves balanced carriers. In such situations, there is no increased risk for Down syndrome in future pregnancies.

Researchers have extensively studied the defects in chromosome 21 that cause Down syndrome. In 88% of cases, the extra copy of chromosome 21 is derived from the mother. In 8% of the cases, the father provided the extra copy of chromosome 21. In the remaining 2% of the cases, Down syndrome is due to mitotic errors, an error in cell division which occurs after fertilization when the sperm and ovum are joined.

Down Syndrome and Maternal Age

Researchers have established that the likelihood that a reproductive cell will contain an extra copy of chromosome 21 increases dramatically as a woman ages. Therefore, an older mother is more likely than a younger mother to have a baby with Down syndrome. However, of the total population, older mothers have fewer babies; about 75% of babies with Down syndrome are born to younger women because more younger women than older women have babies. Only about 9 percent of total pregnancies occur in women 35 years or older each year, but about 25% of babies with Down syndrome are born to women in this age group.

The incidence of Down syndrome rises with increasing maternal age. Many specialists recommend that women who become pregnant at age 35 or older undergo prenatal testing for Down syndrome. The likelihood that a woman under 30 who becomes pregnant will have a baby with Down syndrome is less than 1 in 1,000, but the chance of having a baby with Down syndrome increases to 1 in 400 for women who become pregnant at age 35. The likelihood of Down syndrome continues to increase as a woman ages, so that by age 42, the chance is 1 in 60 that a pregnant woman will have a baby with Down syndrome, and by age 49, the chance is 1 in 12. But using maternal age alone will not detect over 75% of pregnancies that will result in Down syndrome.

The Past, Present, and Future of Down Syndrome

Blythe G. Crissman, Gordon Worley, Nancy Roizen, and Priya S. Kishnani

In this selection four experts focus on the medical advances and social changes that have resulted in an increased life expectancy and quality of medical care in Down syndrome individuals. Blythe G. Crissman is a genetic counselor and research/clinical coordinator of the Duke Comprehensive Down Syndrome Clinic. Gordon Worley is a physician, clinical professor of pediatrics, the director of the Program in Developmental Disabilities at Duke University Medical Center, and codirector of the Duke Comprehensive Down Syndrome Clinic. Nancy Roizen is a physician and chief of the Department of Developmental and Rehabilitation Pediatrics at the Cleveland Clinic Children's Hospital. Priya S. Kishnani is a physician, an associate professor of pediatrics, director of clinical trials in the Division of Medical Genetics at Duke University Medical Center, and codirector of the Duke Comprehensive Down Syndrome Clinic.

SOURCE: Blythe G. Crissman, Gordon Worley, Nancy Roizen, and Priya S. Kishnani, "Current Perspectives on Down Syndrome: Selected Medical and Social Issues," *American Journal of Medical Genetics* Part C (Seminars in Medical Genetics), vol. 142C, 2006, pp. 127–30. Copyright © 2006 by Wiley-Liss, Inc. Reprinted with permission of Wiley-Liss, Inc., a subsidiary of John Wiley & Sons, Inc.

Individuals with Down syndrome (DS) have multiple malformations and have cognitive impairments due to the presence of extra genetic material from chromosome 21. With medical advances, along with improvements in overall care, the median age of death of individuals with DS has increased from 25 years old in 1983 to 49 years old in 1997. This longer life expectancy is providing clinicians with a better understanding of the natural history and the emerging needs of the individual over the lifespan.

Since . . . 1990, there have been many advances in the field. The sequencing of human chromosome 21 has resulted in identification of more than 400 genes on its long arm. Although the genes have been sequenced, defining their roles, functions, and interactions with other genes and the environment will increase our knowledge of the complex phenotype. Understanding the role of genes involved in biochemical/cellular pathways that are relevant to cognition in people with DS will guide future research.

Civil Rights and Down Syndrome

To put this . . . in historical perspective, it is necessary to review briefly the two interwoven strands that together constitute the recent history of DS: the Civil Rights movement for people with disabilities, in which advocacy for people with DS has played an important part, and advances in medical understanding. . . .

Throughout most of history, persons with disabilities have been largely excluded from society, usually living in isolation with their families. Beginning in the 1920s and continuing until the 1960s, parents of children with DS were strongly encouraged by physicians and by society to "place" their children in institutions. This drive to institutionalize people with

FAST FACT

The average life expectancy of an individual with Down syndrome in the United States is 60 years of age.

cognitive disabilities was a part of the Eugenics Movement. The Eugenics Movement had as its main premise that the "race" could be "improved" by preventing "unfit" individuals from "propagating." It reached its culmination in Nazi Germany, with the systematic extermination of people with disabilities, including people with DS, beginning in 1939. After World War II, the Nuremberg Trials of Nazi war criminals established in international jurisprudence the legal principle that everyone in a society is only as safe as the most vulnerable member of the society, providing a legal precedent for protecting people with disabilities. By the 1960s, it was recognized that institutionalization was brutalizing for many people. Scien-

Patients in a mental institution, circa 1946. From the 1920s to the 1960s, parents of children with Down syndrome were urged to send their children to institutions for the mentally disturbed and disabled. (Jerry Cooke/Time & Life Pictures/Getty Images)

tists in 1964 . . . compared institutionalized and home-reared children with DS and demonstrated that home-reared children developed better. In the 1960s and 1970s, the Civil Rights movement for people with disabilities began and flourished. Institutions no longer accepted as many children with disabilities and many adults were "deinstitutionalized" (discharged from institutions). In 1973, the National Down Syndrome Congress (NDSC) was established, and then in 1979, the National Down Syndrome Society (NDSS) was established, both providing support, information, and advocacy for individuals with DS and their families. Legislation began the transformation of educational services for children with disabilities by rejecting the concept of educational segregation for this group of citizens. In 1982, failure to treat a child with DS and duodenal atresia (Baby Jane Doe) led to a new application of the Rehabilitation Act of 1973, rendering discrimination against people with disabilities unacceptable in the provision of medical care, by establishing the right of newborns with disabilities to "customary medical treatment.". . .

Defining Down Syndrome

Most would agree that the beginning of the scientific history of DS was the publication in 1886 of the first complete physical description of the condition by Dr. John Langdon Down. In 1959, Lejeune et al. in France and almost simultaneously Jacobs et al. in England discovered the presence of a third chromosome 21 in DS. Soon thereafter, investigators found that some individuals with DS have chromosomal translocations and others have mosaicism. With the ability to identify DS by karyotype, prenatal diagnosis became a possibility in the 1960s and a reality in the 1970s. The development of an animal model of DS in mice has provided a tool to study deficits in learning, craniofacial maldevelopment, and the neuropathology of Alzheimer disease in DS. The next major breakthrough was in 2000, with the sequencing of chromosome 21. In 2002, scientist Philipp Kapranov and his scientific team described the gene content of chromosome 21. Understanding the effects on protein function of each triplicated gene and how changes in protein function contribute to the phenotype of DS is a work in progress.

Improved Quality of Care

Advances have also been made in the quality of care provided to people with DS. In 1981, physician Mary Coleman presented the first guideline for administering preventive services to people with DS ("Preventative Medicine Checklist"). Professionals and parents now participate in an ongoing process of regularly updating guidelines for the detection and management of the medical, developmental, and behavioral conditions that are more prevalent in DS than in the general population, doing so based on evidence in the literature. Standardization of care by the development of guidelines and their dissemination to practitioners have greatly helped to improve the lives of people with DS and of their families.

The current guidelines emphasize the detection and prevention of secondary morbidities as they arise during the lifespan of people with DS. The conditions for which people with DS are screened vary by age and are different for infants, children, adolescents, young adults, and older adults. Furthermore, the schedule of assessments is often more frequent than that suggested for a typically developing child. In addition, many other conditions are more common in people with DS than in the general population and need to be considered in the differential diagnoses of newly presenting medical problems. The complexity of the screening process is illustrated by a partial list of some of the more common conditions for which it is necessary to screen: congenital heart defects; intestinal atresia; Hitchsprung disease; celiac disease;

The Modern History of Down Syndrome

1920s	Institutionalization is accepted by society as a means to segregate people with DS and other cognitive disabilities.
1941	Nazi Germany begins exterminating people with DS and other disabilities.
1947	The Nuremberg Trials condemn unjust treatment for people with disabilities.
1964	Scientists prove that institutionalization has a negative influence on the development of children with DS.
1960s	The Civil Rights movement begins for people with disabilities.
1970s	Deinstitutionalization becomes public policy. Educational segregation of people with disabilities is declared unlawful. Parents establish the National Down Syndrome Congress (NDSC) and the National Down Syndrome Society (NDSS).
1982	Denial of customary medical treatment to a child with DS and duodenal atresia by parents results in legislation ending the legal basis for discrimination in the provision of medical care to people with DS and other disabilities.
1984	Legislation is passed to facilitate transition from school to employment for people with disabilities.
1985	Early education intervention is demonstrated to be effective in DS. Intervention services for children with DS are expanded by the Individuals with Disabilities Education Act (IDEA).
1992	Legislation to encourage supported employment is passed.
2002	Studies demonstrate that discrepancies by race remain in the care of children with DS.

Taken from: Blythe G. Crissman, Gordon Worley, Nancy Roizen, and Priya S. Kishnani, "Current Perspectives on Down Syndrome: Selected Medical and Social Issues," *American Journal of Medical Genetics*, 2006.

transient myeloproliferative disorders; leukemia; seizures; hypothyroidism; diabetes; atlanto-axial instability and atlanto-occipital subluxation; obstructive sleep apnea; autism and other psychiatric problems; obesity; and cognitive decline.

Even with the use of guidelines, caring for people with DS can be complicated. Over the last 15 years, the number of multidisciplinary, specialized clinics offering care to children with DS has greatly increased. These specialized clinics serve as a resource for primary care physicians and are best utilized by children and adults with secondary conditions requiring the services of a tertiary medical center. . . .

The Future

Improvements in the lives of people with DS will happen as a consequence of many small steps many arenas, including basic science research, clinical applications of scientific advances and in improving opportunities for participation in society. Further work in mouse models of DS will help better understand the phenotype. The development of clinical consortia and multicenter research collaborations will increase the use of evidence-based practices and for conduct of rigorous clinical research which will ultimately advance clinical care.

There is a great deal of work ahead for the promise of an improved quality of life for individuals with DS.

Medical Care and Therapies for People with Down Syndrome

National Institute of Child Health and Human Development

In this selection the National Institute of Child Health and Human Development (NICHD) reviews medical issues associated with a diagnosis of Down syndrome. The organization discusses general and specific health-care needs throughout an individual's lifetime ranging from newborn to pediatric to adolescent to adulthood. The NICHD was initially established to investigate the broad aspects of human development as a means of understanding developmental disabilities, including mental retardation, and the events that occur during pregnancy. Today, the institute conducts and supports research on all stages of human development, from preconception to adulthood, to better understand the health of children, adults, families, and communities.

SOURCE: National Institute of Child Health and Human Development, "Facts About Down Syndrome," nichd.nih.gov, August 18, 2006.

A newborn baby with Down syndrome often has physical features the attending physician will most likely recognize in the delivery room. These may include a flat facial profile, an upward slant to the eye, a short neck, abnormally shaped ears, white spots on the iris of the eye (called Brushfield spots), and a single, deep transverse crease on the palm of the hand. However, a child with Down syndrome may not possess all of these features: some of these features can even be found in the general population.

To confirm the diagnosis, the doctor will request a blood test called a chromosomal karyotype. This involves "growing" the cells from the baby's blood for about two weeks, followed by a microscopic visualization of the chromosomes to determine if extra material from chromosome 21 is present.

When parents are told that their newborn baby has Down syndrome, it is not unusual for them to have feelings of sadness and disappointment. Many parents report that at the time their child is first diagnosed with Down syndrome and during the weeks that follow, they feel overwhelmed by feelings of loss and anxiety. While caring for a child with Down syndrome frequently requires more time and energy, parents of newborn children with Down syndrome should seek the advice of a knowledgeable pediatrician and/or the many Down syndrome support groups and organizations available. . . .

The doctor making the initial diagnosis of Down syndrome has no way of knowing the intellectual or physical capabilities this child, or any other child, may have. Children and adults with Down syndrome have a wide range of abilities. A person with Down syndrome may be very healthy or they may present unusual and demanding medical and social problems at

FAST FACT

There are over fifty clinical signs of Down syndrome, but it is rare to find all or even most of them in one person.

Medical Tests Recommended in Persons with Down Syndrome

Test	Frequency
Hearing exam	Every 2 years
Heart exam	Every year
Dental exam	Twice a year
Mental health exam	Every visit to primary care physician
Nervous system exam	Every year
Eye exam	Every two years
Thyroid tests	Every year
Testicular exam	Every year
Gynecologic exam	Every one to three years (depending on age)

Taken from: W.I. Cohen, ed., "Health Care Guidelines for Individuals with Down Syndrome: 1999 Revision," *Down Syndrome Q*, vol. 4, no. 3, 1999, pp. 1–15.

virtually every stage of life. However, every person with Down syndrome is a unique individual, and not all people with Down syndrome will develop all the medical disorders discussed below.

Down Syndrome and Associated Medical Disorders

During the first days and months of life, some disorders may be immediately diagnosed. Congenital hypothyroidism, characterized by a reduced basal metabolism, an enlargement of the thyroid gland, and disturbances in the autonomic nervous system, occurs slightly more frequently in babies with Down syndrome. A routine blood test for hypothyroidism that is performed on newborns will detect this condition if present.

Several other well-known medical conditions, including hearing loss, congenital heart disease, and vision disorders, are more prevalent among those with Down syndrome.

Recent studies indicate that 66 to 89% of children with Down syndrome have a hearing loss of greater than 15 to 20 decibels in at least one ear, due to the fact that the external ear and the bones of the middle and inner ear may develop differently in children with Down syndrome. Many hearing problems can be corrected. But, because of the high prevalence of hearing loss in children with Down syndrome, an objective measure of hearing should be taken to establish hearing status. In addition to hearing disorders, visual problems also may be present early in life. Cataracts occur in approximately 3% of children with Down syndrome, but can be surgically removed.

Approximately half of the children with Down syndrome have congenital heart disease and associated early onset of pulmonary hypertension, or high blood pressure in the lungs. Echocardiography may be indicated to identify any congenital heart disease. If the defects have been identified before the onset of pulmonary hypertension, surgery has provided favorable results.

Seizure disorders, though less prevalent than some of the other associated medical conditions, still affect between 5 and 13% of individuals with Down syndrome, a 10-fold greater incidence than in the general population. There is an unusually high incidence of infantile spasms or seizures in children less than one year of age, some of which are precipitated by neonatal complications and infections and cardiovascular disease. However, these seizures can be treated with anti-epileptic drugs.

The incidence and severity of these associated medical ailments will vary in babies with Down syndrome and some may require surgery.

Newborns

Babies with Down syndrome often have hypotonia, or poor muscle tone. Because they have a reduced muscle tone and a protruding tongue, feeding babies with Down syndrome usually takes longer. Mothers breast-feeding infants with Down syndrome should seek advice from an expert on breast feeding to make sure the baby is getting sufficient nutrition.

Hypotonia may affect the muscles of the digestive system, in which case constipation may be a problem. Atlantoaxial instability, a malformation of the upper part of the spine located under the base of the skull, is present in some individuals with Down syndrome. This condition can cause spinal cord compression if it is not treated properly.

Infants and Preschool Children

Medical care for infants with Down syndrome should include the same well-baby care that other children receive during the first years of life, as well as attention to some problems that are more common in children with Down syndrome. If heart, digestive, orthopedic or other medical conditions were identified during the neonatal period, these problems should continue to be monitored.

During the early years of life, children with Down syndrome are 10–15 times more likely than other children to develop leukemia, a potentially fatal disease. These children should receive an appropriate cancer therapy, such as chemotherapy. Infants with Down syndrome are also more susceptible to transient myelodysplasia, or the defective development of the spinal cord.

Compared to the general population, individuals with Down syndrome have a 12-fold higher mortality rate from infectious diseases, if these infections are left untreated and unmonitored. These infections are due to abnormalities in their immune systems, usually the t-cell and antibody-mediated immunity functions that

A boy with Down syndrome works with a speech therapist. Speech therapy is one of several programs available to help children with Down syndrome. **(Lauren Shear/Photo Researchers, Inc.)**

fight off infections. Children with Down syndrome are also more likely to develop chronic respiratory infections, middle ear infections, and recurrent tonsillitis. In addition, there is a 62-fold higher incidence of pneumonia in children with Down syndrome than in the general population.

Children with Down syndrome may be developmentally delayed. A child with Down syndrome is often slow to turn over, sit, stand, and respond. This may be related

to the child's poor muscle tone. Development of speech and language abilities may take longer than expected and may not occur as fully as parents would like. However, children with Down syndrome do develop the communication skills they need.

Parents of other children with Down syndrome are often valuable sources of information and support. Parents should keep in mind that children with Down syndrome have a wide range of abilities and talents, and each child develops at his or her own particular pace. It may take children with Down syndrome longer than other children to reach developmental milestones, but many of these milestones will eventually be met. Parents should make a concerted effort not to compare the developmental progress of a child with Down syndrome to the progress of other siblings or even to other children with Down syndrome.

Early Intervention and Education

The term "early intervention" refers to an array of specialized programs and related resources that are made available by health care professionals to the child with Down syndrome. These health care professionals may include special educators, speech therapists, occupational therapists, and social workers. It is recommended that stimulation and encouragement be provided to children with Down syndrome.

The evaluation of early intervention programs for children with Down syndrome is difficult, due to the wide variety of experimental designs used in interventions, the limited existing measures available that chart the progress of disabled infants, and the tremendous variability in the developmental progress among children with Down syndrome, a consequence in part of the many complicating medical factors. While many studies have been conducted to assess the effects of early intervention, the information is limited and contradictory regarding the long-term success of early intervention for children with Down syndrome.

However, federal laws are in place to ensure each state has as a goal that "all handicapped children have available to them a free public education and related services designed to meet their unique needs." The decision of what type of school a child with Down syndrome should attend is an important one, made by the parents in consultation with health and education professionals. A parent must decide between enrolling the child in a school where most of the children do not have disabilities (inclusion) or sending the child to a school for children with special needs. Inclusion has become more common over the past decade.

Adolescence

Like all teenagers, individuals with Down syndrome undergo hormonal changes during adolescence. Therefore, teenagers with Down syndrome should be educated about their sexual drives. Scientists have medical evidence that males with Down syndrome generally have a reduced sperm count and rarely father children. Females with Down syndrome have regular menstrual periods and are capable of becoming pregnant and carrying a baby to term.

Adults with Down Syndrome

The life expectancy for people with Down syndrome has increased substantially. In 1929, the average life span of a person with Down syndrome was nine years. Today, it is common for a person with Down syndrome to live to age fifty and beyond. In addition to living longer, people with Down syndrome are now living fuller, richer lives than ever before as family members and contributors to their community. Many people with Down syndrome form meaningful relationships and eventually marry. Now that people with Down syndrome are living longer, the needs of adults with Down syndrome are receiving greater attention. With assistance from family and caretakers, many adults with Down syndrome have developed the skills required to hold jobs and to live semi-independently.

Premature aging is a characteristic of adults with Down syndrome. In addition, dementia, or memory loss and impaired judgment similar to that occurring in Alzheimer disease patients, may appear in adults with Down syndrome. This condition often occurs when the person is younger than forty years old. Family members and caretakers of an adult with Down syndrome must be prepared to intervene if the individual begins to lose the skills required for independent living. . . .

Future Directions in Down Syndrome Research

Recently, it has been suggested that children with Down syndrome might benefit from medical intervention that includes amino acid supplements and a drug known as Piracetam. Piracetam is a psychoactive drug that some believe may improve cognitive function. However, there have been no controlled clinical studies conducted to date using Piracetam to treat Down syndrome in the U.S. or elsewhere that show its safety and efficacy.

Down syndrome researchers have developed a mouse model to analyze the developmental consequences of Down syndrome. Mice are used because a large stretch of mouse chromosome 16 has many genes in common with those on human chromosome 21. Studying these models at varying stages of development will enhance our basic understanding of Down syndrome and facilitate the development of effective interventions and treatment strategies.

Recent Advances in Research May Lead to New Therapies

Carey Goldberg

In the following selection Cary Goldberg discusses a recent scientific advance in the understanding of the mental retardation found in individuals affected by Down syndrome. This advance is the discovery that a change in a specific gene, called App, appears to cause the mental delays found in Down syndrome. The ability to localize mental retardation to a single gene suggests that a change in that gene or its product could lead to improvements in mental functioning for individuals with Down syndrome. Goldberg is a staff writer for the *Boston Globe*.

Once, the explanation for Down syndrome was simple: You were born with an extra, third copy of the 21st chromosome, with effects ranging from mental retardation to heart problems. Then science began to delve into trickier questions: How, exactly, did

SOURCE: Carey Goldberg, "Research Stirs Hope on Down Syndrome," *Boston Globe*, July 10, 2006. Republished with permission of *Boston Globe*, conveyed through Copyright Clearance Center, Inc.

the extra chromosome act? Which of the hundreds of genes on it mattered, and what did they do?

Now researchers have hopes again for a bit of simplicity. New work in mice suggests that one gene on the chromosome is a major contributor to Down syndrome's learning impairment. And if that's so, then perhaps researchers could devise a treatment targeted at that one gene rather than having to counteract the effects of an entire chromosome.

A Change in Scope

"Some people think, 'My God, you'll never figure it out, you have to get rid of the whole chromosome,'" said Dr. William Mobley of Stanford University, senior author of the paper, which was published in [the first week of July 2006's] issue of *Neuron*. "But it's really possible that beginning with a specific abnormality, you can chase it down—if not to one gene only, then to one gene that plays a major role." And "because you can do that, now you can think about therapies, which you couldn't really do before," he said.

> **FAST FACT**
>
> Chromosome 21 is predicted by scientists to contain between 261 and 364 different genes.

Mobley and others cautioned that a cure for Down syndrome lies far beyond the horizon, but still, they said, such advances in research are cause for hope.

Roger Kafker, a cofounder of the Down Syndrome Research and Treatment Foundation, which helped fund Mobley's work, predicts that such progress might eventually lead to the ability to bring children with Down syndrome up to normal intelligence. It may be wishful thinking, he admits, but he believes that treatment advances could come in time for his 8-year-old son, Michael. "The possibility exists that though you'll never cure the genetic abnormality, that he could learn at a level close to his peer group," Kafker said.

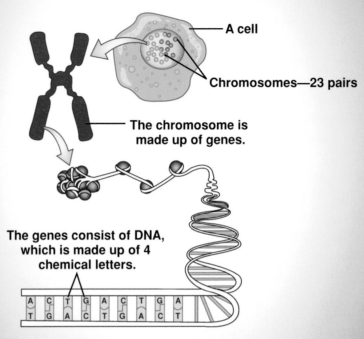

Chromosomes Are Made of Many Different Genes

A cell

Chromosomes—23 pairs

The chromosome is made up of genes.

The genes consist of DNA, which is made up of 4 chemical letters.

A C T G A C T G A
T G A C T G A C T

Taken from: Cancerbackup, "Gene Therapy," September 24, 2007.
www.cancerbackup.org.uk/Treatments/Biologicaltherapies/Genetherapy.

More than 350,000 Americans have Down syndrome and the moderate or mild retardation that generally goes along with it. They are at higher risk for heart defects and childhood leukemia; they are also overwhelmingly prone to develop an Alzheimer's-like dementia by late middle age.

Mouse Models Are the Key

Indeed, the mice used in the *Neuron* research are expected to cast light on what causes brain damage in both Down syndrome and Alzheimer's. They have been genetically engineered to have the kind of triple-chromosome abnormality that Down syndrome causes in humans, including a triple dose of a gene called "App," which instructs the body to make amyloid precursor protein. A piece of that protein, beta-amyloid, accumulates in an abnormal form in the brains of people who have Alzheimer's disease. It appears that having an extra copy of the App gene means more of the protein is produced.

Researchers found that the extra amyloid protein appeared to block a key communication process from neuron to neuron, a message that tells a neuron to "be well, stay alive," as Mobley put it. With that message blocked,

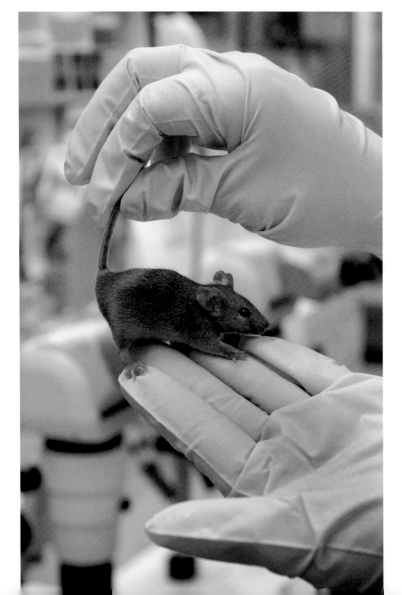

Recent genetic research conducted on laboratory mice like this one indicates that a specific gene may be largely responsible for the learning disabilities suffered by people with Down syndrome. (**AP Images**)

certain neurons important for learning and memory shrivel up.

A Critical Gene

The researchers tested the effect of the amyloid gene several ways and found that the more App a mouse had, the more the communication was blocked. In one key experiment, they created a strain of mice with three copies of chromosome 21 but from which the extra copy of the App gene had been deleted. These mice still had some brain damage, but not as much as the mice with three copies of App.

"It's a very significant step, and it's elegantly done," said David Patterson, a professor and Down syndrome researcher at the University of Denver who was not involved in the *Neuron* paper. "They have shown that the App gene which is present in an extra copy in these mice does cause part of the problem."

"It's not the only thing that causes trouble," he noted, "because if you look at mice in which just the App gene is extra, they only have part of the problem. So there must be other genes, and they don't know what those are. But what they have done here is given us some really good ideas" and "really good targets to pursue."

CHAPTER 2

Controversies in Down Syndrome

Prenatal Testing for Down Syndrome Provides Powerful Knowledge to Parents

Jose C. Florez

In the following selection Jose C. Florez discusses his support of parental choice to learn whether a child is affected by Down syndrome before birth. Through the framework of his personal encounter with a pregnancy at increased risk for Down syndrome, Florez emphasizes that knowledge is power and individual decisions must be supported. However, he also advocates for provision of timely, accurate, and up-to-date information about Down syndrome (and other anomalies) to expectant parents whose fetuses are prenatally diagnosed with Down syndrome. Florez is a physician, director of a clinic for adults with Down syndrome, and the proud brother of a young woman with trisomy 21.

Photo on previous page. Karen Gaskin and her daughter, Lydia, outside Mooreland Elementary School in 1996. It took eight hearings and a state appeal to ensure that Lydia, born with Down syndrome, was mainstreamed for at least one-third of the school day. **(AP Images)**

We were there as beneficiaries of the newly unveiled recommendations of the American College of Obstetricians and Gynecologists,

SOURCE: Jose C. Florez, "Knowledge Is Power," *Journal of the American Medical Association*, vol. 298, October 3, 2007, pp. 1489–90. Copyright © 2007 American Medical Association. All rights reserved. Reproduced by permission.

which now offer prenatal screening for chromosomal anomalies to all couples regardless of maternal age. The physician in both of us firmly held on to the axiom that knowledge is power: as the director of a clinic for adults with Down syndrome and the proud brother of a young woman with trisomy 21, I had encountered many young adults with this condition and had shared so many poignant stories with my wife. Early in this our first pregnancy we had agreed to undergo serum quadruple screening during the second trimester.

The Impact of New Prenatal Testing Recommendations

As it turns out, we had received 10-fold higher odds of having a child with Down syndrome compared to the population average: 1 in 50, rather than 1 in 500 for a woman my wife's age. The genetic counselor had called my wife immediately— sooner than expected, while I was traveling in Europe—and had urged us to schedule this urgent ultrasound. Although the time to detect abnormal nuchal [neck] thickness had passed, it would provide information on any other congenital malformation that may increase our odds. In my absence, my wife's surgical background had helped her keep her composure. On my part, frantic transatlantic telephone calls had vainly tried to soothe; e-mails written with untold emotion could provide only transient comfort.

> **FAST FACT**
>
> The American College of Obstetricians and Gynecologists recommends that testing for Down syndrome should be offered to all women who present for prenatal care before 20 weeks of gestation regardless of maternal age.

Lending a Face to a Diagnosis

Since then, I have often reflected on how my patients who have Down syndrome may view these official recommendations, or their likely outcome. They know.

An ultrasound scan of a fetus during the second to third trimester. Ultrasounds can detect certain malformations that may indicate Down syndrome. (Brigham Narins. Reproduced by permission.)

They question and they may wonder why we think that their lives may be less worth living, when they certainly exult at the chance to be alive and to contribute. Their improved health and remarkable quality of life stand as great accomplishments of modern medicine. As they enjoy the protections of an enlightened culture that welcomes diversity, as they enter a society that more than ever goes overboard to provide services and support to people with disabilities, will they understand the paradox of a door that may not let them in in the first place? I glance at their inquisitive faces and cannot begin to argue cost-benefit societal analyses when the benefits—

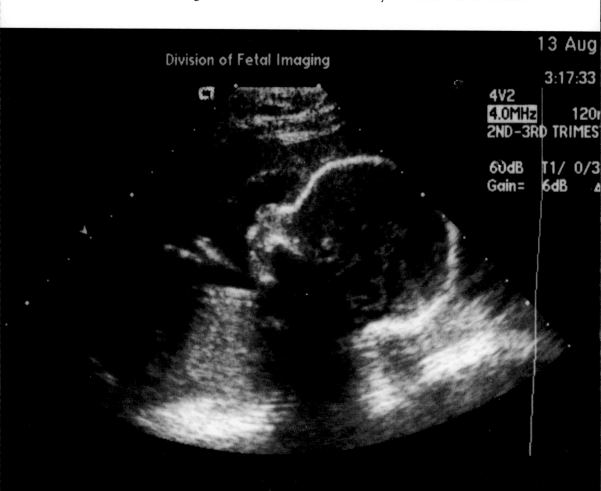

Division of Fetal Imaging

13 Aug

3:17:33

4V2
4.0MHz   120
2ND-3RD TRIMES

60dB   T1/ 0/3
Gain=   6dB

the kindness, affection, delight, innocence, service, tenacity, and loyalty with which they grace us—cannot be quantified. And one fears that, if strength lies in numbers, their dwindling communities will no longer be able to advocate for themselves, while the rest of us will cease to benefit from their presence. . . .

As for me and my wife, the relief afforded by that new information has not made the doubt disappear. The certitude an amniocentesis would yield is not an option for us, because we have decided we cannot place this pregnancy—much desired and long awaited—at risk. But we now face the remaining weeks with the strength and wisdom the fullness of this knowledge has given us. And we relish in the confidence that when Carolina is born, whether she has 46 or 47 chromosomes, she will be welcomed with the unbridled joy she deserves, that joy our obstetrician colleagues and their new parents share every day.

Prenatal Testing Should Not Be Biased Toward Abortion

Patricia E. Bauer

In the following viewpoint Patricia E. Bauer states her concerns that universal prenatal screening for Down syndrome will result in an uninformed intolerance and bias against individuals affected by Down syndrome or other disabilities. She suggests that widespread testing is equivalent to working to eliminate a section of the population, the disabled. Bauer is a journalist and mother of a daughter with Down syndrome.

She was a fresh-faced young woman with a couple of adorable kids, whiling away an hour in the sandbox at the park near my home. So was I, or so I thought. New in town, I had come to the park in hopes of finding some friends for myself and my little ones.

Her eyes flicked over to where my daughter sat, shovel gripped in a tiny fist, and then traveled quickly

SOURCE: Patricia E. Bauer, "What's Lost in Prenatal Testing," *Washington Post*, January 14, 2007, p. B07. Copyright © 2007 The Washington Post Company. Reproduced by permission of the author.

away. The remark that followed was directed to the woman next to her, but her voice carried clearly across the playground. "Isn't it a shame," she said, an eyebrow cocked in Margaret's direction, "that everyone doesn't get amnio?"

Concerns over Expanded Screening

It's been more than 20 years, but I saw the face of that woman again when I read about the recommendation from the American College of Obstetricians and Gynecologists (ACOG) this month [January 2007] that all pregnant women get prenatal screening for Down syndrome. I worry that universal screening brings us all closer to being like that woman at the sandbox—uninformed, judgmental and unable to entertain the possibility that people with disabilities have something to offer.

The ACOG news release notes that the recommendations are based on consistent scientific evidence and will allow obstetricians and gynecologists to best meet their patients' needs. Until now, women 35 or older were automatically offered genetic testing for Down syndrome; under the new guidelines, less invasive and earlier screening options will be extended much more broadly.

What's gone undiscussed in the news coverage of the guidelines seems to be a general assumption that reasonable people would want to screen for Down syndrome. And since nothing can be done to mitigate the effects of an extra 21st chromosome in utero, the further assumption is that people would be reasonable to terminate pregnancies that are so diagnosed.

Certainly, these recommendations will have the effect of accelerating a weeding out of fetuses with Down syndrome that is well underway. There's an estimated 85 to 90 percent termination rate among prenatally diagnosed cases of Down syndrome in this country. With universal screening, the number of terminations will rise. Early screening will allow people to terminate earlier in their pregnancies when it's safer and when their medical status may be unapparent to friends and colleagues.

Passing Judgment

I understand that some people very much want this, but I have to ask: Why? Among the reasons, I believe, is a fundamental societal misperception that the lives of people with intellectual disabilities have no value—that less able somehow equates to less worthy. Like the woman in the park, we're assigning one trait more importance than all the others and making critical decisions based on that judgment.

In so doing, we're causing a broad social effect. We're embarking on the elimination of an entire class of people who have a history of oppression, discrimination and exclusion.

Much of what people think they know about intellectual disabilities is inaccurate and remains rooted in stigma and opinions that were formed when institutionalization was routine. In fact, this wave of terminations and recommendations comes as people with Down syndrome and other intellectual disabilities are better educated and leading longer, healthier and more productive lives than ever.

> **FAST FACT**
>
> Screening for Down syndrome is not 100 percent accurate and may result in false positive or false negative test results.

Nowhere in the fine print of the ACOG recommendations are these misconceptions or the advances of recent years recognized. Perhaps this is not surprising: OB-GYNs concern themselves primarily with mothers and well babies, not people with intellectual disabilities. But it's frightening, too, when you consider the millions of lives affected by their guidance, explicit or otherwise.

Federally funded research has found that physicians have lower expectations for people with intellectual disabilities than do other professionals. Some 81 percent of

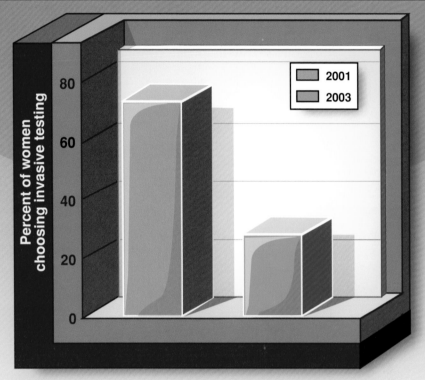

Women over 35 Years of Age Who Chose Invasive Procedures Before and After the Availability of Noninvasive First Trimester Screening in 2003

Percent of women choosing invasive testing

2001
2003

80
60
40
20
0

Taken from: Andrea M. Wray et al., "The Impact of First-Trimester Screening on AMA Patients' Uptake of Invasive Testing," *Prenatal Diagnosis*, vol. 25, no. 5, 2005, pp. 350–53.

medical students polled by Special Olympics in 2005 said that they are "not getting any clinical training" about people with intellectual disabilities. The Hastings Center found that 80 percent of genetics professionals polled said they personally would terminate a pregnancy involving Down syndrome. These are the people advising pregnant women in the harried days when the clock is ticking.

A Wish

Here's my fervent hope: that calls for universal prenatal screening will be joined by an equally strong call for providing comprehensive information to prospective parents, not just about the tests but also about the rich and rewarding lives that are possible with disabilities. If physicians and genetics professionals are willing to learn from people with disabilities and their families, they can disseminate the nuanced, compassionate message at the

Universal prenatal screening may cause some parents who would have had a Down syndrome child to terminate the pregnancy. Many people feel that people with intellectual disabilities can lead fulfilling lives and make contributions to society. (**Steve Dunwell/The Image Bank/Getty Images**)

core of diversity and human rights: All people have value and dignity and are worthy of celebration.

Plastic shovels no longer captivate Margaret. She's more interested in her school roommates, her part-time job, the Red Sox and, at least recently, wrestling on TV. She knows how to hold an audience and how to bring down the house with a one-liner. And, like most of my relatives, she knows how to be an absolute pill some of the time. Such is life.

That day in the sandbox, I went home and cried. I didn't know what to say. I didn't know whether the woman was right. Today, I know. She was wrong.

Most Children with Down Syndrome Should Be Educated in Integrated Classrooms

National Down Syndrome Society

In the following viewpoint the National Down Syndrome Society presents the benefits of inclusive education. The authors define inclusive education as the practice of welcoming, valuing, empowering, and supporting diverse academic and social learning among students of all abilities. They feel that inclusive education is effective, beneficial, and valuable for all parties: disabled students and standard students. The National Down Syndrome Society was founded to benefit people with Down syndrome and their families through national leadership in education, research, and advocacy.

In a growing number of schools across the United States, it is now possible to walk into elementary, middle and secondary classrooms and observe students with Down syndrome and other cognitive and physical disabilities learning with their nondisabled peers. This

SOURCE: National Down Syndrome Society, "Inclusion," ndss.org, 2007. Reproduced by permission.

practice of welcoming, valuing, empowering and supporting diverse academic and social learning among students of all abilities is called inclusive education.

Inclusive education is more than mainstreaming. Mainstreaming implies that a student from a separate special education class visits the regular classroom for specific, usually non-academic, subjects. Inclusion is an educational process by which all students, including those with disabilities, are educated together for the majority of the school day. With sufficient support, students participate in age-appropriate, general education programs in their neighborhood schools.

Inclusion is a philosophy of education based on the belief in every person's inherent right to fully participate in society. Inclusion implies acceptance of differences. It makes room for the person who would otherwise be excluded from the educational experiences that are fundamental to every student's development.

FAST FACT

Down syndrome children in mainstream schools have a higher academic performance than those in segregated classrooms.

When inclusion is effectively implemented, research has demonstrated academic and social benefits for all students: both those who have special needs as well as typical students. Friendships develop, nondisabled students are more appreciative of differences and students with disabilities are more motivated. True acceptance of diversity ultimately develops within the school environment and is then carried into the home, workplace and community.

While inclusive education is a highly effective educational approach—a fact that has been recognized for decades in federal disability rights and education laws—some students with special needs may benefit from other arrangements. There are many educational strategies and placements available to students with Down syndrome, including self-contained special education classes, resource rooms, mainstreaming, residential schooling and home instruction. . . .

A Brief History of Inclusion

Until the late 1970s, students with disabilities were routinely placed in segregated educational settings, such as separate specialized schools or institutions. In 1970, schools in the United States served only one in five students with special needs. Since then, researchers, policy makers, parents and educators have debated how to integrate special and general education services into one educational system that serves all students. Educational practices such as mainstreaming, the "regular education initiative" and inclusion have shown that all students of differing abilities benefit from learning together.

Federal law followed parents' growing demand for education of their children with disabilities in more inclusive settings. Established to grant states federal money to educate children with disabilities, the Education for All Handicapped Children Act was instituted in 1975. Later renamed the Individuals with Disabilities Education Act (IDEA) in 1990, this law sought to end segregation and exclusion of this group from general education settings. IDEA mandated that a "free and appropriate public education" be available to all school-age children with special needs, regardless of disability. An amendment in 1986 added children three to five years of age.

In 1985 U.S. Assistant Secretary of Special Education Madeleine Will introduced the Regular Education Initiative [REI], named to convey the notion that students with mild disabilities could participate in the general education program at their neighborhood school. Not long afterward, advocacy efforts expanded the REI concept to include students with moderate and severe disabilities.

By 1990, this concept was further expanded and renamed "inclusive schooling" or "inclusion," the practice of welcoming all students into general education class-

rooms in their neighborhood schools with the necessary support, services, and curricular and instructional modifications. By 1993, almost every state was implementing inclusion at some level.

A nondisabled girl works with a boy with Down syndrome in a mainstreamed classroom. (© Ellen Senis/The Image Works)

Today, the inclusion discussion has expanded beyond special education and has become part of the total school reform movement. Reports like Winners All, published in 1992 by the National Association of State Boards of Education, demonstrated success in inclusive schools and urged states to adopt a new inclusive belief system, re-train teachers and revise funding formulas to support inclusive educational practices. . . .

Key Court Decisions

Since the passage of IDEA in 1975, numerous federal court cases have affirmed the right of students with Down syndrome and other disabilities to attend regular classes. The courts continue to clarify the intent of this law. For example, in 1983, the *Roncker v. Walter* case addressed the issue of "bringing educational services to the child" versus "bringing the child to the services." This case established another principle of inclusion: portability. If special education services can be successfully delivered in a general education classroom, the law says it is inappropriate to offer such services in a segregated setting. They are also referred to as "pull-in" services.

In 1988, the U.S. Court of Appeals ruled in favor of Timothy W., a student with severe disabilities whose school district contended he was "too disabled" to be entitled to an education. The ruling against the school's position clarified the school district's legal responsibility under IDEA to educate all children with disabilities in the least restrictive environment, without exception. . . .

In 1993, the U.S. Court of Appeals for the Third Circuit upheld the right of Rafael Oberti, a child with Down syndrome, to be educated in his neighborhood school with adequate and necessary support services. . . . The court placed the burden of proof for compliance with IDEA's requirements squarely upon the school district and the state rather than the family. The Oberti decision established another important rule: that the school cannot justify a more restrictive placement on the basis that the student would make greater educational progress in that setting. As long as the student is getting some educational benefit in inclusion, the argument of greater educational benefit elsewhere will not affect placement. This rule is extremely important because many educators assume that a student with Down syndrome will learn more academics in a segregated setting. This assumption is often untrue and it does not take into consideration the non-academic benefits of inclusion.

Other cases clarified a fourth factor: cost. In order for cost to affect an LRE [least restrictive enviroment] decision, it has to be so high as to "significantly impact" the education of other students. In 1994, the U.S. Court of Appeals for the Ninth Circuit upheld the district court decision in *Holland v. Sacramento Unified School District* that indicated inclusion is the presumed starting point for placement of children with disabilities. The court found that the school district exaggerated the costs of educating Rachel Holland by attributing expenditures to her that would also benefit other students (e.g. training and paraprofessional support).

Advocates of inclusion often cite parallels to other struggles for human and civil rights, all of which have emphasized that legal, moral or philosophical segregation

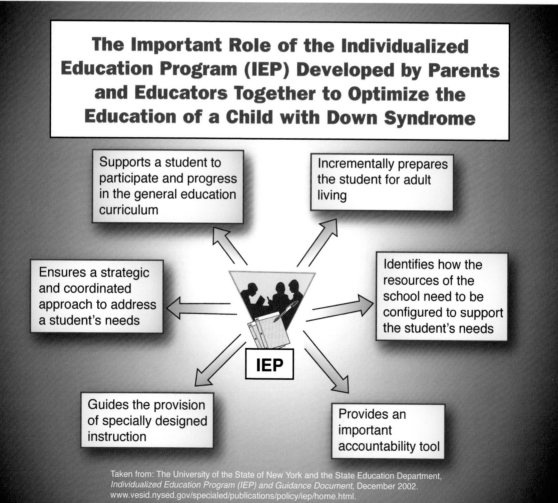

The Important Role of the Individualized Education Program (IEP) Developed by Parents and Educators Together to Optimize the Education of a Child with Down Syndrome

Supports a student to participate and progress in the general education curriculum

Incrementally prepares the student for adult living

Ensures a strategic and coordinated approach to address a student's needs

Identifies how the resources of the school need to be configured to support the student's needs

IEP

Guides the provision of specially designed instruction

Provides an important accountability tool

Taken from: The University of the State of New York and the State Education Department, *Individualized Education Program (IEP) and Guidance Document*, December 2002. www.vesid.nysed.gov/specialed/publications/policy/iep/home.html.

of subgroups of people is a violation of civil rights and the principle of equal citizenship. Many believe Chief Justice Earl Warren clarified this in the landmark *Brown v. Board of Education* decision more than four decades ago. The decision indicated that imposing separateness in education can generate a feeling of inferiority so deep that it can permanently interfere with a student's motivation to learn and grow.

Benefits of Inclusion

Several years ago, the basic premise of special education was that students with disabilities would benefit from a unique body of knowledge and from smaller classes staffed by specially trained teachers using special teaching materials. While the premise remains valid, there is no compelling evidence demonstrating that segregated special education programs have significant benefits for students.

A number of studies over the years have reported the various benefits of inclusive education. In 1996, the National Down Syndrome Society published a research report on the inclusion of children with Down syndrome in general education classes. After analyzing and comparing extensive parent and teacher questionnaires, this study found that with proper support and adequate communication between parents, teachers and professionals, inclusion is a favorable educational placement for children with Down syndrome. The study also found that the learning characteristics of students with special needs were more similar to their nondisabled peers than they were different. Moreover, teachers reported positive experiences with students with Down syndrome. They described their students as eager to learn, especially when encouraged, and reported personal satisfaction in terms of their professional achievements. . . .

In May 2000, the Indiana Inclusion Study investigated the academic benefits of inclusive education for students without disabilities. This study concluded that students without disabilities who were educated in inclusive settings made significantly greater progress in math than their peers. Although their progress in reading was not significantly greater than their peers, there was a "consistent pattern" in their scores that favored educating students without disabilities in inclusive settings.

This and other research has highlighted improved academic skills, social skills, communication skills and peer relationships as four of the most important benefits of inclusion. Nondisabled students can serve as positive speech and behavior role models for those with disabilities and students with disabilities offer their nondisabled peers acceptance, tolerance, patience and friendship. As allies and friends, peers can offer support both in and out of the classroom. These findings show that everyone involved in inclusive schooling can benefit from the experience.

The introduction to the Individuals with Disabilities Education Act acknowledges that education in inclusive settings works when the mandates of the law are followed. It states:

Over 20 years of research and experience has demonstrated that the education of children with disabilities can be made more effective by:

Having high expectations for such children and ensuring their access to the general education curriculum to the maximum extent possible; Strengthening the role of parents and ensuring that families of such children have meaningful opportunities to participate in the education of their children; Providing appropriate special education and related services, aides and supports in the regular classroom to such children, whenever possible; and Supporting high-quality intensive professional development for professionals who work with such children.

Inclusive education has also been shown to have a positive impact on employment outcomes. A 1988 study . . . , spanning fifteen years, found that students with disabilities educated in inclusive settings had an employment rate of 73 percent while those in segregated programs had an employment rate of 53 percent. . . . [Another study in 1989] found that the more time students with disabilities spent in regular classes, the more they achieved as adults in employment and continuing education. More recently, in its 1997 annual report to Congress, the U.S. Department of Education noted: "across a number of analyses of post-school results, the message was the same: those who spent more time in regular education experienced better results after high school." As nearly all employment settings are themselves inclusive, involving people with and without disabilities, it is easy to imagine why inclusive education has a positive impact on employment outcomes.

Overcoming Barriers

Many children with disabilities continue to be educated in separate classrooms or schools for all or most of the day, even when their parents believe an inclusive setting would be more appropriate.

Why does this happen? Researchers have identified a variety of perceptual, cultural and emotional barriers that cause people to resist the idea of students with and without disabilities sharing the same classroom. In some cases the barrier is simply a matter of prejudice. But there are also many more complex views, including the belief that only those students with disabilities who are closer to "normal" can or should be included and the belief that the needs of students with disabilities are unique and beyond the reach of general educators.

Others may be concerned about the need for special expertise to support the student's academic and social learning or the potential for students with disabilities to disrupt the classroom. Concerns may also include the costs associated with special services and the idea that functional life skills cannot be addressed in general classroom settings.

Successful inclusion programs allay these concerns. In fact, models of inclusive education can be models for the education of all students, as they overcome barriers and offer a variety of approaches which reach a broader range of students and improve learning. These successful inclusion programs demonstrate how certain changes in the structure of school systems, classroom operations and the roles of teachers, students, parents and community members can enable equal access to general education curricula and related services for all students.

The Future of Inclusion

Tremendous progress has been made since the passage of the first special education law in 1975 to guarantee students with disabilities full educational rights and opportunities. These advances would not have been possible without the parents of children with disabilities and, increasingly, the individuals with disabilities themselves, who have always been the most visionary, vocal and effective advocates of the inclusion movement.

It is the parents and self-advocates who have rejected institutional placement, started the first schools for students with moderate and severe disabilities and mounted national advocacy campaigns to secure the federal laws that brought us mainstreaming and later inclusion.

It is understandable that families have led the movement because inclusion is not just about philosophy, educational practices or legal statutes. Inclusion is about children and their families—their dreams and their futures.

Mainstreaming Does Not Meet the Social Needs of All Children with Down Syndrome

Amy Dockser Marcus

In the following viewpoint Amy Dockser Marcus argues that integrated classrooms cannot always meet the social needs of disabled students, as individual teens can feel isolated from their average peers in a regular classroom. She emphasizes her point through the story of a teen with Down syndrome who chose to leave an inclusive education setting in favor of a segregated classroom with other disabled students. Marcus's position is that as students continue to resist inclusion, more disabled students may take the initiative to leave the mainstream and rejoin special education classrooms. Marcus is a staff reporter for the *Wall Street Journal*.

For years, Eli Lewis was the only student in his class with Down syndrome. The genetic condition, which causes a range of cognitive and physical impairments, made it harder for him to do his school work. But his parents felt strongly that he could succeed. They

SOURCE: Amy Dockser Marcus, "Eli's Choice," *Wall Street Journal*, December 31, 2005. Reprinted with permission of the *Wall Street Journal*, conveyed through Copyright Clearance Center, Inc.

hired a reading tutor. An aide worked with his teachers to modify tests and lessons so that he could be in the same classroom as everyone else. He participated in his middle school's award-winning chorus and was treated as a valued member.

But when all the other kids in his class were making plans to go to the local high school this fall, Eli, 14 years old, said he didn't want to go. He wanted to be in a small class with other students like him. "I don't want to get lost in a big crowd," Eli says.

Eli's declaration surprised his parents. Then his mother recalled the many times she stopped by the school to check on her son, only to find him eating by himself. Once, when she came to pick him up from a dinner that chorus members attended, she says she found Eli sitting with his aide, while the other students sat at a different table.

"The kids liked him, they knew him, they spoke to him," says his mother, Mary Ann Dawedeit. "They just didn't think of him as a peer." Eli, she says, was tired of "being the only kid who was different."

Federal law mandated in the 1970s that children with disabilities be offered a "free and appropriate public education" in the "least restrictive environment," rather than being separated only in special schools or institutions. Over the years, advocacy and additional laws resulted in efforts to get children with disabilities placed in regular classrooms, with proper support, whenever possible. The process, called "inclusion" or "mainstreaming," has largely been an academic success.

Sometimes the Academic Benefits Are Not Enough

Studies have shown benefits for all children, not only those with disabilities, who study together. Many researchers argue this is one reason why people with Down syndrome have made such remarkable progress in recent decades. People with Down syndrome who learn in regular classrooms do much better academically, research has found. They also have significantly higher rates of employment after they graduate and earn more money than peers who studied mainly in self-contained classes.

And yet, Eli Lewis's experience poses a difficult dilemma, one that is only now starting to be recognized and addressed. With help, he had succeeded academically in a regular classroom. But he felt isolated. In a book . . . published [in 2006], researchers at the Center for Social Development and Education at the University of Massachusetts in Boston say that although people with intellectual disabilities made enormous gains academically due to inclusion, their social integration at school "remains stagnant."

In a survey of 5,600 seventh- and eighth-grade students from 70 schools across the country, more than half of the youths said they were willing to interact with students with intellectual disabilities at school. But only one-third said they would be willing to invite such students to their house or go to the movies with them, according to the survey done by the University of Massachusetts center and the Washington-based opinion firm, ORC Macro. "Student attitudes continue to remain the most formidable barrier to inclusion," the researchers concluded.

FAST FACT

Nearly 2.9 million students are currently receiving special education services for learning disabilities in the United States.

At first, Ms. Dawedeit and her husband, Howard Lewis, thought Eli might change his mind. The couple—who have two other sons who don't have Down syndrome—felt there were many advantages to Eli staying in a regular classroom, including greater independence and more interaction with the general student body. But eventually, Mr. Lewis says he began to recognize that having Eli in a regular classroom might not be "as important to Eli as it is to me."

Ms. Dawedeit remained reluctant. She talked with a friend who had a son with Down syndrome, who was also learning in a regular classroom. "I felt like I had let her down," Ms. Dawedeit says. "I had preached a mantra for so long to so many."

In May [2005], at the science exposition at Eli's middle school, her feelings changed. The eighth-graders took over the school hallway and parents were invited to visit. Some students demonstrated elaborate experiments they had been working on. Eli worked with his aide to do research online about the chemical properties of silver. He learned where to find it on the periodic table. For the exposition, he printed out some of the documents he had found.

When his mother came to see his project, Eli again raised the subject of where he was going to high school. For Ms. Dawedeit, the contrast was sharp. Here was Eli, successfully participating in a science exposition with peers who didn't have disabilities—but still talking about wanting to be with other people with Down syndrome. She says she realized she needed to try to accommodate her son's desire for a social group. "I really had to step back from my personal beliefs," she says.

In the fall, Eli enrolled in the ninth grade at Bethesda's Walter Johnson High School, a sprawling building of over 2,000 students. He is in a special program with 20 other students who have disabilities, including one who gets around in a wheelchair and has difficulty talking. Six of the students in the class have Down syndrome. Eli already knew some of the kids from various extracurricular activities, such as drama class and Special Olympics, where he participated in soccer, basketball, swimming and bowling.

Returning to Segregation

Getting out of the mainstream has meant trade-offs. His school is about 10 miles from Eli's house, farther than the local high school that his older brother attends. (The local high school doesn't have a separate special-education program.) A special-education bus now comes each day to pick up Eli, along with other students with disabilities. "This was one of our big compromises," says his mother. In middle school, Eli walked to a bus stop and rode a regular school bus. "Other kids knew him," says Ms. Dawedeit. "Now he's a special-ed kid on a bus."

One evening in November, after a dinner of chicken burritos and salad, Eli helped his brothers, ages 12 and 17, clear the dishes. Then his parents watched him, as he started making his way through his homework—a worksheet to practice using nouns and verbs. Since Eli was born, they had fought to have him included in regular classrooms. Now it sometimes felt as if Eli might end up outside the world they had tried so hard to keep him in.

All along, they shared a similar goal: for their son to be able to live independently. But Mr. Lewis, a lawyer, began to worry that the academic gap between Eli and other classmates was getting wider in the regular classroom as he grew older, and might be too difficult to bridge in high school. "I'm not married to inclusion at the expense of Eli's getting the skills he needs," he says.

Ms. Dawedeit, a manager at a retail store, was less certain. She knew how much Eli, like all kids his age, wanted to belong. But without spending significant amounts of time in regular classrooms, how would he ever learn the skills he needed to reach the goal of living on his own? "The truth is he has to go out and get a job," she says. "If he's educated with his regular peers, then maybe a regular peer will hire him."

Eli finished his English worksheet, and got up to take a break. He came over and gave his father a hug. "Are you meeting any new kids at school, Eli?" his dad asked. "Not just yet, Dad," Eli answered. "Why are you hanging out only with the kids in your class?" his father queried. "Because I know them," Eli answered, and went into the kitchen to get some cookies.

At his new school, the Parent Teacher Student Association has put the issue of how to promote the inclusion of students with disabilities in extra-curricular activities on the agenda for its January meeting. A student group that pairs students with disabilities with a buddy without disabilities has already scheduled several activities for the coming months, including ice skating and bowling.

Still, for most of his school day, Eli is now in a separate classroom from the general school population. Last month, ninth-graders in the general-education classes

Eli Lewis (left) and his family stand in front of Walter Johnson High School, where he transferred so that he could be in a special program with other students with disabilities. (Jeff Hutchens/Getty Images)

were reading the novel, "To Kill a Mockingbird." In the special-education classroom, the teacher was going over worksheets that had been adapted from the book, with some related questions.

Eli was signed up for a regular physical-education class, but asked his parents if he could switch to one with only special-education students. His mother was reluctant to change, because it was one of his only chances to meet kids in the general-student population. She offered a compromise: He could switch to the special-education gym class with his friends, if next semester he took weight-training as part of the regular class. Eli agreed.

Challenges for Schools

Janan Slough, the assistant principal who oversees the special-education department at Eli's school, says the school has difficulty finding certified special-education teachers because of a national shortage. The school tries to foster as many opportunities as possible for those with disabilities to be in general classrooms, she says. Still, she adds, "I feel caught" between juggling the need for socializing with the need to teach basic, crucial tasks, such as handling money. On one field trip, the special-education kids went to a grocery store; they were supposed to buy something their family might use at home, pay for it, and make sure they got correct change.

Most of the kids with disabilities need to focus on independent-living and job skills, rather than college preparation. "I'm charged with thinking about where they are going to be at 21," she says. "I don't want parents to come back and say, 'It's nice they were socially included and had parallel instruction, but you didn't prepare them for the world of work.'"

From Normal Inclusion

For now, Eli has only one class—ceramics—that he attends with the general school population. On a recent morning, Eli sat next to a boy assigned to help him. The students were designing tiles, and from time to time his peer assistant would look at what he was doing, or go with him to get more clay. For much of the class, the boy bantered with one of his friends, who had pulled up a chair next to him and was regaling him with a story. From time to time, Eli made a joke and the boys all laughed together. But when they walked Eli back to the special-education classroom, there was no suggestion that they meet up again that day. When Eli was asked if he enjoyed spending time with his assigned partner, he shrugged and said, "It's OK."

Eli has a lot of ideas about what he wants to do after high school. In middle school, he took a media class and worked in the school's TV studio. Along with the other kids in the class, he was given a homework assignment to make a public-service announcement. Eli made one about the Special Olympics. "I want to be a director," he said, when asked about his plans after high school.

"Eli has serious career aspirations for himself that may not have anything to do with what the rest of the world sees for him after high school," said his mother, one afternoon last month, while waiting for him at a drama class he takes outside of school. The class, made up of students with and without disabilities, was planning a variety show, and Eli was excited about performing. Every night, he went to his room to work on a dance routine he had created to accompany a song from the soundtrack of the movie, "Holes."

His girlfriend, whom he met in elementary school and also has Down syndrome, had invited him to be her date to the upcoming Winter Ball at her private school. Next month, Eli will turn 15 and is planning a big party. The only kids he plans to invite also have disabilities, his mother says.

While she's glad he has found a social circle, she still wonders about what he's missing by going to

College Opportunities Expand for Disabled Students

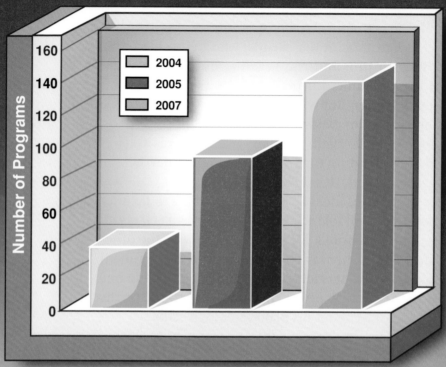

Taken from: Rubin and Aduroja, "College Opportunities Expand for Disabled," *Chicago Tribune,* December 11, 2005, and *Kansas City Star,* "National Down Syndrome Congress Convention in KC Shows How Times Have Changed," August 5, 2007.

special-education classes instead of staying in regular classes. "I go back and forth on it all the time," she says. For instance, his school has a state-of-the-art TV studio with editing facilities and a control room, where a class is given. Eli's parents wanted him to be in that class, but it's not possible right now, because he needs to attend the special-education math class, which is held during the same period.

On a recent morning at school, Eli weaved around the teenagers lining the hallway. Some sprawled on the floor, catching up on homework. Others joked with each other by their lockers, or rushed to get to their next class. Eli didn't talk to any of the students. He walked with purpose, heading to the special-education room.

When he got there, his face brightened when he saw one of his friends. "This is my best friend," he said, throwing his arm around the other boy, who also has Down syndrome. He pressed his face close to his friend's until their cheeks almost touched. Eli smiled. "What table are you sitting at lunch today?" he said as they walked together down the hall. "Come on, make sure you sit with me."

Sterilization Should Be an Option for Down Syndrome Individuals

Hoangmai H. Pham and Barron H. Lerner

In this selection Hoangmai H. Pham and Barron H. Lerner discuss their position that current laws prohibiting the sterilization of the developmentally disabled without a court decision is overprotective and needlessly complicated. Using a Down syndrome case example, the authors enumerate the ways in which barriers to sterilization of an individual labeled mentally unable to decide for themselves can results in harm to the affected person and cause undue burden to family members. When coauthoring this article, Pham was the Jay I. Meltzer ethics fellow at Columbia University and Lerner was an Angelica Berne Gold Foundation fellow.

A century ago, the eugenics movement led to widespread forced sterilization of vulnerable populations. Subsequent moral outrage produced laws that strongly discouraged or prohibited sterilization of the developmentally disabled. Ironically, this legacy may represent a burden for developmentally disabled women today.

We present a fictionalized case of a developmentally disabled woman whose guardian requests surgical sterilization. We review the historical factors that have shaped relevant legal boundaries and discuss medical and ethical issues confronting clinicians in such a situation. We argue that current restrictions on sterilization may be overprotective, thus denying the "best interests" of patients and their families.

Case History

Carla is a 24-year-old woman with Down syndrome. She has an IQ of 40. Carla lives with her grandfather and legal guardian, Henry, and has never been institutionalized. Her parents died when she was an infant, and she has no other immediate family. She attends a special needs school.

Carla's medical history includes successful repair of a congenital atrioventricular canal malformation, mild pulmonary hypertension detected echocardiographically, and asthma for which she needs regular use of bronchodilators. Breast development and secondary hair growth are normal.

Carla menstruates monthly and needs assistance to manage her menstrual hygiene. According to psychosocial evaluations, she remains naive about sexuality. Henry keeps Carla out of sex education classes. Carla consistently refuses pelvic examinations because teachers told her "not to lie down with strangers."

Henry now asks Carla's internist about bilateral tubal ligation for his granddaughter. He broaches sterilization for the first time because of his own age and poor health and because of his concern that after he dies, Carla would not get her current level of supervision.

Henry is particularly concerned about sexual assault. He insists on sterilization rather than reversible contraception because he believes Carla would require less monitoring afterward. He worries that the potential medical complications of pregnancy, "could kill" Carla and that life would be "much harder" for her with a baby because future caretakers might not want to be responsible for both mother and child. Henry chose a niece to assume guardianship of Carla after his death but is uncomfortable relying on such a distant relative. Carla does not answer when asked whether she knows she can have babies or if she wants to have a child.

Historical Background

American eugenicists argued that forced sterilization was in society's best interest. Inspired by the social Darwinism propounded by Francis Galton, many concluded that social ills could result from characteristics transmitted genetically among "unfit" populations. They believed that "defective" people reproduced at higher rates, that criminals and the developmentally disabled tended to have children with similar disorders, and that reproduction among these populations weakened the gene pool.

In 1907, reflecting the eugenicists' influence, states began enacting laws allowing involuntary sterilization of the developmentally disabled. Courts initially declared early sterilization statutes unconstitutional, but support for such legislation grew after World War I.

Forced sterilization fell out of favor after 1940 as Nazi atrocities led to a rejection of eugenic tenets and later due to growing support for civil rights and feminism. In the 1960s, some states repealed sterilization laws. Finally, a scandal involving the sterilization of a developmentally disabled girl without her consent in a federally funded clinic resulted in 1978 guidelines that forbade the use of federal funds for sterilizing anyone younger than 21 years, incompetent, or institutionalized. . . .

Given the current legal landscape, it remains extremely difficult to obtain sterilization for an incompetent woman. In Illinois, parents of incompetent children can request sterilization unless challenged by a third party. In other states, courts will not approve sterilization for incompetent persons without enabling legislation. Some states mandate court review and approval for each case. In New York City, the charter forbids sterilization of people younger than 21 years or incompetent. In 2 instances, New York State allowed sterilization of minors: 1 suffering from painful menses, and the other deemed "unlikely ever to understand . . . contraception, [who] could be psychologically traumatized if she became pregnant, . . . gave birth or had pregnancy terminated, and [could] participate in . . . sexual activities or have . . . [them] . . . imposed on her."

Francis Galton was an early supporter of eugenics. This movement sought to improve society through genetic intervention. (**Hulton Archive/Getty Images**)

But parents of adult incompetent women cannot consent by proxy for sterilization.

Carla's physician, in consultation with the hospital's legal counsel, advises Henry that local courts would likely refuse petitions to request sterilization.

Ethical Framework

Legal prohibitions do not relieve clinicians of responsibility for considering relevant medical and ethical issues and from advocating for patients.

Bioethicists generally approve of surrogates making decisions for incompetent patients. Courts have recognized that incompetent, developmentally disabled persons must have others make medical decisions for them. In Carla's case, the severity of her Down syndrome leads to a court determination that she is incompetent. Henry is appointed her legal guardian. In making decisions for people who have never had capacity, surrogates rely on the best-interest standard. This standard assesses risks and benefits of proposed treatment alternatives, including pain and suffering, and improvement or loss of functioning. Ethical dilemmas may emerge if providers or the state objects to decisions made by surrogates.

We draw on Carla's case to suggest that laws designed to protect incompetent people from coercive sterilization may actually infringe on their rights. Courts that allow proxy consent for sterilizations have proposed the following common guidelines. These are consistent with the ethical framework above and with recommendations by the American Academy of Pediatrics and the American College of Obstetricians and Gynecologists that have attempted to outline rational sterilization policies.

Guidelines for Proxy Consent Sterilization

The patient is permanently incompetent and a court-appointed guardian represents her in full judicial hearings. Carla's mental disability is permanent. She cannot consent voluntarily because she cannot understand the risks and benefits of various alternatives. Henry would have to give proxy consent. Some legal scholars suggest that a court-appointed advocate charged with the responsibility of arguing against sterilization during judicial review would be an important procedural safeguard.

The patient undergoes medical, psychological, and social evaluations. Henry remains willing for Carla to undergo additional evaluations as necessary.

The patient can reproduce but cannot care for offspring. Carla could not care for a child alone. . . . Although only some 30 pregnancies in women with Down syndrome have been reported, low pregnancy rates may reflect social and behavioral factors. Furthermore, the majority of these pregnancies resulted in live births. Carla could conceive and give birth. She is unlikely to engage in intercourse voluntarily, but her risk of being sexually assaulted is substantial. Forty percent of 104 developmentally disabled women referred to a gynecology clinic were suspected or confirmed victims of such abuse. How many pregnancies result from such assaults is not known. Guidelines on sterilization of developmentally disabled women recommend sexual-abuse avoidance counseling, but this recommendation does not reassure Henry that after he dies, Carla would not be exposed to more people, less supervision, and greater risk.

Sterilization is in the patient's best interest, and she is allowed to express her understanding and opinion of the procedure. Henry does not seek sterilization to treat menometrorrhagia or myomas; some states allow sterilization under such circumstances. Instead, for Carla, we must weigh risks and benefits of tubal ligation versus pregnancy. Pregnancy has potential benefits. Carla appreciates the nurturing bond with her grandfather. She might desire to possess a baby, without understanding reproduction. We cannot predict her potential fulfillment in birthing or seeing a child grow, which weighs against the irreversible decision to sterilize her.

Another argument against sterilization is that it deprives patients of sexual autonomy, important in the movement to "mainstream" the developmentally disabled. Rights of self-determination, including that of procreative choice, are constitutionally protected, but exercising those rights requires "knowledge and ability to exercise [them] freely." Given that a surrogate would have to facilitate an incompetent patient's right to procreate, how meaningful is the notion of sexual autonomy in such a circumstance? To a large extent, Carla's sexual autonomy was already curtailed when she was denied sex education and told to "never lie down with strangers." Although families disagree about the wisdom of shielding children from information about sex, we are reluctant to interfere in such family decisions. That caretakers could thus curtail Carla's sexual activity calls into question why sterilization becomes the crucial decision point.

We rightly approach invasive interventions with caution but should recognize that less dramatic actions, although engendering little scrutiny, may effectively render patients "infertile" by proxy consent.

Moreover, procreative choice includes both the right to refuse sterilization and the right to choose it. . . . Blanket prohibitions against sterilization of the mentally incompetent may violate this right. New Jersey's Supreme Court came to the same conclusion in 1979 when it allowed proxy consent for sterilization of an incompetent, developmentally disabled woman. The irreversibility of sterilization, however, does obligate us to more rigorously ensure that it is in a patient's best interests.

> **FAST FACT**
>
> In 1981 the New Jersey Supreme Court concluded that the fight to prevent conception through sterilization is one of the privacy rights protected by the U.S. Constitution that should not be discarded for the mentally retarded solely on the basis that their condition prevents conscious exercise of choice.

What are the medical risks? Carla's pulmonary hypertension and asthma raise the possibility of perinatal cardiopulmonary complications. Labor and delivery also tend to be harder for developmentally disabled women because of pelvic abnormalities and difficulty cooperating with instructions. Late detection of pregnancy might result in delayed prenatal care. We can only speculate about the psychological risks of pregnancy, birth, or abortion, and the morbidity and mortality risks of pregnancy in any woman are higher than those associated with laparoscopic tubal ligation. . . .

When it comes to sterilization, however, laws supplant subjective consideration of quality-of-life concerns in individual cases. Should we not apply the same ethical standard to proxy decisions for reproductive health as for any other medical issue?

Sterilization is the most practical, least restrictive contraception available. Henry dismisses Carla's use of other contraceptive methods after he dies. Compliance issues rule out barrier methods and lack of adequate supervision would prohibit the use of hormonal contraceptives. Although an intrauterine device is long lasting and has minimal risks, Henry worries that complications might occur. He worries about Carla being traumatized by repeated pelvic examinations that require sedation and about Carla's need for supervision should complications occur or when replacement became necessary.

Motivations for requesting sterilization are examined. We must ask what secondary gains might be involved and whether they are in conflict with patients' best interests. Such discussions are invaluable for exploring relevant family concerns.

A survey of 88 parents found that 75 (85%) were willing to consider sterilization for their developmentally disabled children; 8 (10%) requested it. Parents cited fear about the efficacy of other methods and about pregnancy, particularly from sexual abuse—reasons similar to those

The Benefits and Drawbacks of Contraception Methods for Women with Down Syndrome

Method	Benefits	Drawback
Depo-Provera Contraceptive Injection (Depot Medroxyprogesterone Acetate)	Simple Effective Protects against pregnancy for 3 months	• Injection • Possibly decreased bone mineral density • Weight gain • Possible breakthrough bleeding
"The Pill" containing Progestin taken 21 days a month	Oral route Effective	• Possibly decreased bone mineral density • Weight gain • Possible breakthrough bleeding • Dependant on regularly taking a pill the same time every day
"The Pill" containing Estrogen and Progestin taken continuously	Oral pill	• Periods reduced, not eliminated • Risk of blood clots • Concerns about increased breast and cervical cancer risk
Lupron injections [a gonadotropin-releasing hormone antagonist (GnRH antagonist)]	Highly effective	• Injection • Decreased bone density concerns • Expensive • Menopause symptoms • Sterile abscess • Polycystic ovary concerns
Mirena or other Intrauterine system (IUS) or Intrauterine device (IUD)	No systemic drugs	• Invasive • Periods reduced, not eliminated • Infection • Device expulsion
Removing the lining of the uterus (endometrical ablation)	Less invasive than hysterectomy	• Invasive • Ethical and legal concerns • Poor efficacy • May require repeat procedures • Potential for permanent sterility • No pregnancy prevention effect
Removing the uterus (hysterectomy)	Highly effective	• Major surgery • Permanent sterility • Ethical and legal concerns

Taken from: Albanese and Hopper Archives of Disease in Childhood 2007; 92:629–632.

Henry expresses. Few thought their children could want or care for a child. Perhaps most instructive, 85 (97%) said they would want medical staff to help them make the decision but not to decide for them.

Henry first requests sterilization after Carla is well into her reproductive years. Henry seems less concerned with his own convenience than with Carla's welfare after his death. His decision appears to reflect his sincere assessment of Carla's best interests.

Families Should Have a Voice

Laws forbidding sterilization of the mentally incompetent may be nearly as dehumanizing as the forced sterilization laws they replaced. Weighing the complex medical and ethical issues involved, judging whether guardians' fears are reasonable, and determining patients' best interests require careful, individual case reviews with strict procedural safeguards. Families are often the best substitute voice for incompetent adults. Not allowing a caring family to express preferences regarding such life-altering experiences as pregnancy and childbirth may paradoxically silence the patient's voice.

Sterilization Takes Away Basic Human Rights

Disabled Peoples' International

In the following position statement Disabled Peoples' International strongly condemns forced sterilization of any individuals, including those with disabilities. The organization believes that forced sterilization is an act of dehumanizing violence and abuse that denies disabled individuals their basic human rights to bodily integrity and to either father or bear children. Disabled Peoples' International is a network of national organizations or assemblies of disabled people, established to promote human rights of disabled people through full participation, equalization of opportunity, and development.

D isabled Peoples' International (DPI) is a cross-disability network of national organizations or assemblies of persons with disabilities, established to promote the human rights of persons with dis-

SOURCE: "DPI (Draft) Position Statement on Forced Sterilization of Persons with Disabilities," Disabled Peoples' International, http://v1.dpi.org, May 1, 2007. Reproduced by permission.

abilities through full participation, equalization of opportunity, equalization of outcomes, and development. DPI and its member organizations are built on principles of dignity and justice, and the concepts of inalienability, universality and indivisibility of human rights.

Oregon governor John Kitzhaber signs a declaration in 2002 proclaiming December 10th as Human Rights Day. He also apologized to the Oregonians—more than twenty-five hundred girls in reform schools, poor women, and the mentally disabled—who were among those who underwent involuntary sterilization between 1917 and 1983. (AP Images)

Universal Rights for the Disabled

In keeping with the following Articles of the United Nations Convention on the Rights of Persons with Disabilities:

• Article 4—General Obligations to ensure and promote the full realization of all human rights and fundamental freedoms for all persons with disabilities without discrimination of any kind on the basis of disability;

States That Performed Sterilization Programs Until 1956

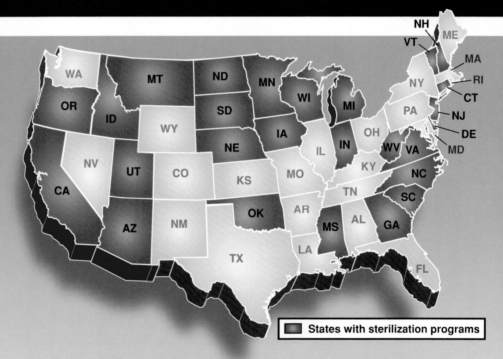

States with sterilization programs

Taken from: Robert Proctor, *Racial Hygiene: Medicine Under the Nazis.* Cambridge, MA: Harvard University Press, 1988, and Gisela Bock, "Nazi Sterilization and Reproductive Policies," in Dieter Kintz, ed., *Deadly Medicine: Creating the Master Race.* Washington DC: U.S. Holocaust Memorial Museum, 2004.

- Article 5—Equality and Non-discrimination recognizing that all persons are equal before and under the law and entitled without discrimination to the equal protection and benefit of the law;

- Article 16—Freedom from Exploitation, Violence and Abuse entrenched through legislative, administrative, social, educational, monitoring and other measures;

> **FAST FACT**
>
> In the first half of the 20th century, thirty-three states in the U.S. mandated the sterilization of over sixty-five thousand people who were thought to be carriers of defective genes.

- Article 23—Respect for Home and the Family through measures to eliminate discrimination in all matters relating to marriage, family, parenthood and relationships on an equal basis with others, ensuring among others, the rights to marry, to found a family, to decide freely and responsibly on the number and spacing of children, and to retain fertility.

A Call for Further Legislation

DPI believes that forced sterilization is an act of dehumanizing violence and abuse that denies individuals their basic human rights to bodily integrity and to either father or bear children, and is in violation of the above Articles.

DPI believes that forced sterilization may result in adverse life-long physical and mental health impacts on the individual.

DPI condemns forced sterilization of all girls and boys, women and men, whether they have a disability or not, as a gross infringement of their human rights and the U.N. Convention on the Rights of Persons with Disabilities.

DPI calls on governments of the world to develop universal legislation that prohibits forced sterilization of girls and boys, women and men, particularly persons with disabilities as per our mandate.

CHAPTER 3

Personal Perspectives on Down Syndrome

I Am a Person with Lots of Plans

Eleanor Bailey

In this viewpoint eleven-year-old Eleanor describes her emotions upon learning at school that she has a label; Down syndrome. Eleanor is sad and scared to learn about her label; she does not want to be labeled or have Down syndrome. However, through discussions about Down syndrome with her mother, her friends at school, and her friends at the the Association for Persons with Severe Handicaps (TASH) convention, Eleanor decides that she is still the same person with many future plans, even if she has a label.

I am 11 years old and in fourth grade. This year some little girls came to my school. I heard some people say they had Down Syndrome. On a Saturday I asked my Mom, "Do I have Down Syndrome?" Mom said that I do.

I went to my bedroom and closed the door. I didn't cry but I shut the door and was mad and upset. I didn't want to have Down Syndrome.

Photo on facing page. Four siblings, one with Down syndrome, embrace in a group hug. (Realistic Reflections/Getty Images)

SOURCE: Eleanor Bailey, "Eleanor Helps Herself," *Mouth*, March, 2000. Reproduced by permission.

My Friends and Teacher Still Like Me

On Monday I went to school. I told my teacher, Mrs. Karr, that I had an announcement to make. She gave me the microphone and I said: "I have two things to say. First, I have Down Syndrome and second, I am really scared that none of you will like me anymore."

My friends were really nice. They said they already knew that and they still liked me. Some of them cried. I got lots of hugs.

But I am still not happy!

On Wednesday my Dad and I got on an airplane and went to Chicago. On the airplane I listened to my Walk Man. I have a song that goes, "Clang, clang, rattle, bing, bang, I make my noise all day." I thought that is what I can do. Even with Down Syndrome I can still make my noise.

Trying to Get Rid of Down Syndrome

We went to the Association for Persons with Severe Handicaps [TASH] Convention. There were lots of really cool people there. We stayed in a big hotel. In our room there were two bathrooms. One had a shower and one had a bathtub. I made a sign that said "Girls" and put it on the door of the one with the bathtub. I didn't want my Dad to come in.

I took lots of baths. I thought if I took enough baths I could wash my Down Syndrome away. I also thought I would put hair spray on it but my Mom and Dad won't let me have hair spray. I tried to put sun screen on it because I thought that maybe then I wouldn't have to have it all of the time. But my Dad said that none of that would work.

Successful Friends with Disabilities

I have friends that were at TASH. My really special friend is Tia Nelis. She lives in Illinois. Tia has a disability but when she talks people listen. They really listen. Tia is a leader and she really likes me. I told Tia that I have Down Syndrome. I was surprised when she said that she has always known that. She said she didn't care. She said that I am an important person and that Down Syndrome is not as important as being a wonderful person. When I grow up I want to be just like Tia!

I have other friends at TASH who told me the same thing. I met a really nice person named Katie. Katie goes to college. She has Down Syndrome. I also talked to my other friend Liz Obermayer. Liz has a new job and is moving to Maryland which is a state. Liz has a disability but she is a leader too. She is on the Board of TASH. Liz goes to lots of meetings and people listen to her too.

Finding Role Models

I got my name from Eleanor Roosevelt. Lots of bad things happened in her life. I have read all about her. She

Actor Chris Burke, foreground left, holds a torch and helps lead the third annual Buddy Walk in Anderson, South Carolina. The Buddy Walk raises money for awareness and acceptance of Down syndrome across the country. Eleanor Bailey, now an adult and an activist for Down syndrome awareness, has been a featured speaker at this event. (**AP Images**)

was a leader. I also know about Rosa Parks, Martin Luther King, Nelson Mandela and Robert Kennedy. Lots of bad things happened to them but they were strong and were leaders. My Dad says they made people proud of who they are and made them free.

I Have Lots of Plans

I wish I didn't have Down Syndrome. But I do and I am a person with lots of plans.

When I wonder what to do I remember my song. I will do what it says. I will go "clang, clang, rattle, bing, bang" and make my noise all day. Even though I am sad I know I can be as tough as anyone. That is what I want to do.

Just be me.

I Am Like Other Teens

Melissa Riggio and Rachel Buchholz

In this viewpoint Melissa Riggio, as told to Rachel Buchholz, discusses the basics of Down syndrome and then describes her full life as a teenager affected by Down syndrome. She emphasizes that people with Down syndrome are much like people without Down syndrome, with unique strengths and talents. Riggio is a high school senior affected by Down syndrome. Buchholz is a writer and senior editor of *National Geographic Kids* magazine.

W hen I first started to work on this story, I thought maybe I shouldn't do it. I thought you might see that I have Down syndrome, and that you wouldn't like me. My mom thinks that's silly. "Have you ever met anyone who didn't like you because you have Down syndrome?" she asks me. She's right, of course. (She usually is!)

SOURCE: Melissa Riggio and Rachel Buchholz, "I Have Down Syndrome: Know Me Before You Judge Me," *National Geographic Kids*, December, 2006, pp. 34–37. Copyright © 2006 National Geographic Society. Reproduced by permission.

When people ask me what Down syndrome is, I tell them it's an extra chromosome. A doctor would tell you the extra chromosome causes an intellectual disability that makes it harder for me to learn things. (For instance, some of my classes are in a "resource room," where kids with many kinds of learning disabilities are taught at a different pace.)

When my mom first told me I had Down syndrome, I worried that people might think I wasn't as smart as they were, or that I talked or looked different. I just want to be like everyone else, so sometimes I wish I could give back the extra chromosome. But having Down syndrome is what makes me "me." And I'm proud of who I am. I'm a hard worker, a good person, and I care about my friends.

A Lot Like You

Even though I have Down syndrome, my life is a lot like yours. I read books and watch TV. I listen to music with my friends. I'm on the swim team and in chorus at school. I think about the future, like who I'll marry. And I get along with my sisters—except when they take my CDs without asking!

Some of my classes are with typical kids, and some are with kids with learning disabilities. I have an aide who goes with me to my harder classes, like math and biology. She helps me take notes and gives me tips on how I should study for tests. It really helps, but I also challenge myself to do well. For instance, my goal was to be in a typical English class by 12th grade. That's exactly what happened this year!

But sometimes it's hard being with typical kids. For instance, I don't drive, but a lot of kids in my school do. I don't know if I'll ever be able to, and that's hard to accept.

> **FAST FACT**
>
> Down syndrome children benefit from music, dance, and other arts programs.

My Dream to Be a Singer

I try not to let things like that upset me and just think of all the good things in my life. Like that I've published two songs. One of my favorite things to do is write poetry, and this singer my dad knows recorded some of my poems as singles.

Right now someone else is singing my songs, but someday, I want to be the one singing. I know it's going to happen, because I've seen it. One day I looked in the mirror, and I saw someone in my head, a famous person

Selena Waters, a high school student with Down syndrome and member of the girls' basketball team, celebrates after scoring. (**AP Images**)

or someone who was somebody, and I just knew: I will be a singer.

It's true that I don't learn some things as fast as other people. But that won't stop me from trying. I just know that if I work really hard and be myself, I can do almost anything.

See Me as an Individual

But I still have to remind myself all the time that it really is OK to just be myself. Sometimes all I see—all I think other people see—is the outside of me, not the inside. And I really want people to go in there and see what I'm all about.

Maybe that's why I write poetry—so people can find out who I really am. My poems are all about my feelings: when I hope, when I hurt. I'm not sure where the ideas come from—I just look them up in my head. It's like I have this gut feeling that comes out of me and onto the paper.

I can't change that I have Down syndrome, but one thing I would change is how people think of me. I'd tell them: Judge me as a whole person, not just the person you see. Treat me with respect, and accept me for who I am. Most important, just be my friend.

After all, I would do the same for you.

What Is Down Syndrome?

Down syndrome is an intellectual disability that about 5,000 babies in the United States are born with each year. A person with Down syndrome has 47 chromosomes, microscopic structures that carry genetic information to determine almost everything about a person. Most people have only 46 chromosomes. It's the extra chromosome that can cause certain physical characteristics (such as short stature and an upward slant to the eyes) and speech and developmental delays. Still, people with Down syndrome are a lot like you: They are unique people with strengths and talents.

An Unexpected Blessing

John C. McGinley, with Lori Berger

In the following viewpoint writer Lori Berger tells John C. McGinley's story about his son Max who was diagnosed at birth with Down syndrome. McGinley allows a candid glimpse into the initial reaction to an unexpected diagnosis of Down syndrome in a child and the path to acceptance and love. McGinley is an actor best known for his role on the TV show *Scrubs*. Berger writes for magazines and is editor in chief of the teen magazine *Jump*.

M y favorite John Lennon quote is, "Life is what happens to you while you're busy making other plans." That could have been the banner across my house on August 30, 1997, the day our baby was born. From everything the obstetrician had told us, my wife, Lauren, and I were expecting a healthy baby girl. We had done all the tests, except an amniocentesis. We'd decided against it because we were told that the chances of losing

SOURCE: *Redbook*, v. 204, June 2005. Copyright © Hearst Communications, Inc. All rights reserved. Reproduced by permission.

the baby were about 1 in 250, and that scared us. I had waited a long time to meet someone I could marry and have children with, and I didn't want anything to go wrong. But what happened sure wasn't the fairy-tale scenario I'd had in my head.

On that August day when Max came out, it was like a giant cosmic hammer slammed us on the head. First off, the baby girl we were expecting turned out to be a boy.

Actor John C. McGinley poses for photos after reading to a group of children with Down syndrome. McGinley's own son, Max, also has Down syndrome. (Chad Buchanan/Getty Images)

Then the nurses took Max into the NICU [Neonatal Intensive Care Unit] and the pediatrician pulled me aside. She told me that Max had markers—like dots on his irises, and a crease on his hand called a simian crease (a term so archaic it pains me to say it—that indicated he had Down syndrome. At that moment, I didn't fully comprehend what it meant. I just knew Max was going to have challenges, and that this wasn't going to be the Norman Rockwell version of family life that I had imagined.

> ## FAST FACT
> Down syndrome often originates from an event that occurs during the formation of the reproductive egg or sperm.

I could not process what was going on, other than to give Lauren as much support as possible. One of the first people who came to see us that day—I assume he was dispatched by the state or the hospital—was some guy who informed us, "The state will take your child if you don't want him." It was horrible, but it just made Lauren and me circle the wagons and pull them in tighter around our son.

We soon learned that Max had a health problem to battle, too. He was born with microscopic holes in his heart, a not uncommon complication of DS (Down syndrome). So Lauren and I stayed in the NICU for the first weeks of his life, rotating shifts. Fortunately, after six weeks, Max's condition self-corrected, and we were able to take him home.

Waiting and Hoping

Those first few months, Lauren and I beat ourselves up, wondering, What did I do to bring this on? You talk to the shrink, you talk to the doctors, and you slowly embrace the fact that sometimes these things just happen. Then one day, you walk into your child's room and look down at him, and he's staring back at you with a look that says, What about me? And suddenly your "burden" is transformed into a gift. And you just start giving, everything you've ever had inside and even more, from places you never knew you had. And then it's just love, love, and more love.

So here I was finally having this love affair with my son, when God dealt him another challenge: a seizure disorder. Over the next two years, the doctors tried everything to cure his seizures, but nothing worked. Then, miraculously, when Max was around 3, the seizures just stopped.

Father-Son Fun

I really bonded with Maxie post-seizures. I would come back from work and just want to eat him up because he was such a total cuddle bunny. I also had more to contribute as Max became more of a little boy. Once I could play with Max on the jungle gym or take him to the beach to run with our dogs, it started to strengthen his core. Slowly but surely, walking became running and running led to jumping.

And fortunately, the gene pool that spawned him gave him a double dose of stubborn. That's become an asset and a liability, because when he wants to accomplish something, it's stunning what he's capable of—but when he doesn't want to do something, he's not going to do it. Max has been on an explosive growth curve since the age of 3. He's now 7 1/2 and he's become this precocious menace to society. His fine and gross motor skills are off the charts. Right now, we're focusing on his verbal communication. We had him in a special-needs preschool, but we've switched him to an inclusive program at a regular school, where he's happy and doing great.

Now that Max is in school, I lose sleep thinking about whether he is being teased. Down syndrome or not, kids pick on each other. My pet peeve is the use of the word "retard." It's about excluding people. And by perpetuating all that negativity about what these kids can't do, you're excluding them and limiting what they can accomplish. I'm shooting commercials for NBC to raise awareness of this issue.

I'm also the spokesperson for the National Down Syndrome Society's Buddy Walk program. There are hundreds of walks around the country in October; they're a chance for the parents to feel supported and the kids to come out and play.

Lauren and I—who are no longer married but are still best friends—consider ourselves blessed. I used to think I knew what love was before Max, but when I put him to bed and he wraps his arms around me and whispers, "Good night, Daddy, love you,"—and he's just strung together this sentence after years of work—I feel so much love. And it hits me: This is truly as good as life gets. Thanks to Max, I have much more patience, but the converse of that is I have no patience for people who don't appreciate their blessings.

Sure, I get tired sometimes. Special needs or not, kids run you into the ground. But I've never felt once that Max was draining. He feels like an energy source to me. After a weekend with him, I've inhaled so much Maxie love that I'm able to come to the set of *Scrubs* and function from love. It sounds absurd coming out of my mouth—I'm Mr. Caustically Acerbic—but a kinder, gentler soul—since the introduction of Max into my world.

Other parents of children with Down syndrome seek me out because they know about Max, but I don't have any solid answers for them, except: Show up, be compassionate, tell the truth, and give love. And, actually, that's what all parents have to do.

My Child Has Unlimited Potential

In the following viewpoint Sue Mayer discusses the birth and child-hood of her son Sam who has Down syndrome. Sue recounts Sam's diagnosis with Down syndrome at birth, his medical issues during the first year of life, and his numerous therapies. She notes that having Sam has taught her never to take the simple things in life for granted. Mayer is the mother of three children including Sam. She also founded the Wisconsin chapter of the National Association for Child Development.

My pregnancy and labor were textbook normal, all my tests came back in the normal range, but everything quickly changed when Sam was born. The nurses were huddled around him; he was put on oxygen and then taken to the nursery for additional care. This is what my husband and I were told at least. I knew something was wrong as soon as I overheard that

SOURCE: Sue Mayer, "Sam's Journey to 'Reach for the Stars,'" *EP Magazine*, February, 2007 pp. 34–36. Reproduced by permission.

our pediatrician was on his way. The panic quickly began to take root and rise.

Dr. Montgomery walked in and closed the door, it was at that moment I began to cry and knew that something was wrong with Sam. The doctor's explanation was thorough and complete, but what I will remember is the compassion in his voice, his gentle nature and the time he spent with us and our family to help answer our questions and concerns.

The next 48 hours were filled with tears, medical tests, grief, disbelief (he doesn't look like he has Down syndrome) and uncertainty of his future—uncertainty that we, as parents, could handle all of this. Finally, we were given some hope and were allowed to hold Sam for the first time. I looked at Sam and cried tears of joy and tears of concern. I had wondered during that first 24 hours if he would look at me or right past me. Sam looked directly at me. My husband, Jeff, and I held him and talked about everything we were thinking, good and bad, our hopes and our concerns. It was at that point we started to accept the diagnosis, accept that we could not change it and that we needed to start thinking about how to move on. When I got home, I contacted the Birth to 3 program in our home state of Wisconsin, a program that offers early intervention for children from birth to age 3. I also began interviewing clinics and spent hours reading books and doing research on the Internet.

Medical Issues

I wish I could say that Sam's first year was uneventful and that everything went as we hoped. Instead, we coped with a lot of respiratory illnesses and found it difficult to keep Sam healthy and out of the pediatrician's office. Sam was hospitalized twice for bronchiolitis and pneumonia. He stopped breathing on three separate occasions, which required him to be put in the intensive care unit (ICU), and we had our first trip via ambulance. We had an apnea monitor installed as well as sleep and swallow studies. Jeff and I got very little sleep because of the need to continuously reposition Sam to assist with his airway through the night. At 11 months, Sam had his tonsils and adenoids removed, which helped a great deal. I was concerned that all of his illnesses and hospitalizations were going to cause further delays. I began to feel that the Birth to 3 program was not going to be enough to help Sam reach his potential, whatever that potential may be.

Therapy

I enjoyed working with Sam's therapists and felt they were a group of caring professionals, but I just had a feeling that we needed to do more. I went back to my Internet research and came across a letter written to the parents of children with Down syndrome by Robert J. Doman, Jr., founder of the National Association of Child Development (NACD). In that letter, Mr. Doman told me my child has unlimited potential. I was sure my prayers had been answered. Sam was 18 months old when we had our first evaluation. He was not crawling, he could not chew, and he was also using repetitive body movements, also called self-stimulating, by dangling socks and rocking to and fro.

Our evaluator told us to build a ramp. We did and within two weeks Sam was crawling in a beautiful cross crawl pattern. From that point on things just took off.

Through this wonderful organization, NACD, I have been taught how to work with Sam one-on-one with a 2–3 hour daily program. NACD's programs are based on the philosophy that all children—challenged, typical or gifted—can learn faster and accomplish more if they are provided with the opportunity. The key to success is parental involvement. NACD has over its twenty years of existence and through its work with 25,000 clients, devel-

> **FAST FACT**
>
> Development in Down syndrome children may be enhanced through regular physical therapy and exercise.

oped a unique and effective view and approach to enhancing the development and function of children and adults.

Sam's program is unique to him and addresses all areas of his development including physical, fine and gross motor skills, speech, oral motor, cognitive processing and learning, mobility, tactility, nutrition and behavior. NACD programs are designed to address and eliminate each of the child's specific problems. This is accomplished by a series of daily activities, tasks and training sessions that are developed after a thorough

A mother holds her son, who has Down syndrome. (AP Images)

evaluation. Once a program is designed, it is worked on daily under the direction of the parent and with the help and support of NACD staff and their international network of parents. The key is NACD's innovative approaches and eclectic treatment. NACD's staff and international network are on the cutting edge of human development and education.

What has Sam accomplished with the help of NACD? Sam was fully potty trained even through the night, at the age of 3. Sam began word reading at the age of 3 and now, at age 5, is able to read well over 600 words along with beginning readers. Sam knows the names and sounds of the alphabet. He can identify shapes, colors and can count to ten. Sam can identify 125 species of animals and 40 different types of tools and their uses. While Sam was also diagnosed with apraxia, a type of speech disorder, he has now begun to speak in two and three word sentences.

"Children with significant problems can be typical, typical children can be exceptional and exceptional children can change the world," said Doman. "At NACD we are working to help the children and change the world."

It was my dream to start a Wisconsin Chapter of NACD and that dream was realized in March 2006 when the first set of evaluations for the Wisconsin Chapter were conducted in Port Washington, Wisconsin. Currently, our chapter is working to produce a calendar that will be presented during a legislative brunch next year in order to introduce our state representatives to our program, our children and our families. We hope to start the process of getting state funding for our families in the program. We are also working on fundraising as well as developing brochures for new parents and a website.

All my children have their strengths and their weaknesses. Our journey with Sam has taught us to never take a developmental milestone for granted. Hard work does pay off: patience and persistence are key. Sam has taught us much: live life to the fullest, smile as much as you can, laugh from your soul, never take for granted the little things in life, and each and every day give someone a hug and let them know you love them. Only time will tell where Sam's journey will lead us next, but I look forward to it and embrace each day knowing that he will continue to amaze, teach and empower me to help him reach his full potential.

My Brother Jacob Is Special

Sarah Baltisberger

In the following viewpoint Sarah Baltisberger discusses her feelings about having a brother with Down syndrome. She feels lucky to have her brother and his unique and special gifts in her family. Sarah Baltisberger is a fifth grader from Ohio.

My little two-year-old brother Jacob has Down Syndrome. It is a disability, but people with Down Syndrome have many special abilities. People with Down Syndrome are born with an extra chromosome in every cell of their bodies.

When Jacob was born, I was really excited. I went to the hospital room and held him with so many happy feelings. Then, I went home and my mom called and told me that Jacob had Down Syndrome. It felt like all the good feelings went away. But now, I realize that there is

SOURCE: Sarah Baltisberger, "My Brother Jacob is Special," *Skipping Stones*, vol. 16, June–August 2004, p. 11. Copyright © 2004 *Skipping Stones*. Reproduced by permission.

nothing different about Jacob, he is a normal brother; he just has a different path through life. I wouldn't want to change anything about Jacob because he is very special to me. I think it is a miracle that Jacob is alive!

Jacob has some unique gifts. He is one of the happiest people in my life! Now, when I see or hear about a person with Down Syndrome, I think, "Wow, was that family blessed."

Jacob loves baths, but he doesn't like to get out of the bath. He loves getting messy eating spaghetti. He puts tomato sauce in his hair! Jacob also loves books, just like I did when I was little. Occasionally, he rips a few pages, but we can always tape them back together.

Jacob makes me smile, even when I have a lot of homework or a headache. He is someone I never thought would come into my life, and I'm very thankful to have him!

Jacob uses sign language to express his feelings and needs. Jacob loves Mom, Dad, Anna and me. He doesn't just sign it—he really means it.

I know Jacob can do anything! I will be his cheerleader. I believe in Jacob. I believe in angels. I believe that some angels don't have wings.

FAST FACT

According to the *American Journal of Medicine*, Down syndrome children generally have a positive impact on their siblings.

GLOSSARY

amniocentesis   A diagnostic procedure usually performed at around fifteen to twenty weeks of pregnancy. The test involves removing a small amount of the fluid surrounding the fetus in the womb. This fluid contains cells and proteins that can be analyzed in order to diagnosis certain genetic disorders, birth defects, and chromosomal conditions.

chorionic villus sampling (CVS)   A diagnostic procedure usually performed at around ten to twelve weeks of pregnancy. It involves removal of placental cells surrounding an embryo in order to diagnose certain genetic disorders and chromosomal conditions before birth.

chromosome   A cell part that contains genetic information. Average humans have twenty-three pairs of chromosomes, one member of each pair inherited from the mother, the other from the father.

congenital heart defects   Heart defects that are present at birth.

developmental delay   A term used to describe individuals who are behind schedule in reaching milestones of early childhood development.

first trimester screening   Testing between eleven and fourteen weeks of pregnancy that assesses fetal risk of having chromosomal anomalies. These screening tests only predict the risk for chromosomal changes and cannot definitively diagnosis a baby with a chromosomal abnormality.

gene   The basic unit of inheritance. Genes, which are found on the chromosomes, determine the structure and function of all components of the body.

hypotonic   A term used to describe decreased muscle tone or strength. It is often described as floppiness.

mental retardation	A term used when a person has certain limitations in mental functioning and in skills such as communicating, taking care of him- or herself, and social skills.
prenatal	A term referring to the period before birth.
second trimester screening	Maternal serum screening tests, also known as the "triple screen" or "quad screen," measure chemicals in the mother's blood between sixteen and twenty weeks of pregnancy in order to assess the fetal risk for chromosomal anomalies and certain birth defects. These screening tests only predict the risk for chromosomal changes and cannot definitively diagnose a baby with a chromosomal abnormality.
trisomy	The presence of three copies of a chromosome rather than the standard two.
ultrasound	A procedure using high frequency sound waves to examine a fetus for anomalies and abnormal development.

CHRONOLOGY

1838 French psychiatrist Jean-Étienne Dominique Esquirol describes the physical appearance of a child with Down syndrome.

1844 Edouard Séguin publishes a clinical description of Down syndrome.

1866 British physician John Langdon Haydon Down describes the clinical features of Down syndrome.

1920 Institutionalization becomes accepted by society as a means to segregate people with Down syndrome and other cognitive disabilities from the general population.

1933 Scientists demonstrate that the most significant risk factor for Down syndrome is advanced maternal age, not paternal age or birth order.

1941 Nazi Germany begins a program to exterminate people with Down syndrome and other disabilities.

1947 The Nuremberg Trials, a series of trials that included the prosecution of prominent members of the political, military, and economic leadership of Nazi Germany, condemn unjust treatment of people with Down syndrome and other disabilities.

1948 The link between Down syndrome and Alzheimer's disease is recognized in North America by physician George A. Jervis.

1959 The cause of Down syndrome is linked to an extra chromosome in the 21st pair of chromosomes (trisomy 21).

1961 A group of nineteen geneticists write to the editor of the medical journal *Lancet* suggesting that the term "mongolian idiocy" should be changed. The *Lancet* supported the name Down's Syndrome. The National Association for Down Syndrome [NADS] is founded by parents who chose to go against medical advice and raised their children with Down syndrome at home.

1964 D.J. Stedman and D.H. Eichorn prove that institutionalization has a negative influence on the development of children with Down syndrome.

1965 The World Health Organization (WHO) officially drops references to "mongolism" as requested by the Mongolian delegate.

1970s Laws are passed to recommend people with disabilities be integrated into the community rather than sequestered in institutions (deinstitutionalization).

1971 Prenatal diagnosis for Down syndrome and other chromosomal anomalies is introduced and becomes available to the general public.

1973 Parents establish the National Down Syndrome Congress (NDSC).

1975 Educational segregation of people with disabilities is declared unlawful through Public Law 94-142. The National Institutes of Health convenes a conference to standardize the nomenclature of genetic conditions and malformations. They recommend eliminating the possessive form "Down's Syndrome" and using exclusively "Down syndrome" to describe trisomy 21.

1979 Parents found the National Down Syndrome Society (NDSS).

1981 A U.S. physician develops the first Down syndrome specific preventive medicine checklist that addresses the medical care of individuals with Down syndrome.

1982 A parental decision to decline routine medical treatment to correct an intestinal defect of a child with Down syndrome, called duodenal atresia, results in legislation ending the legal basis for discrimination in the provision of medical care to people with Down syndrome and other disabilities.

1984 Legislation passes to facilitate transition from school to employment for people with disabilities

1985 A study is published demonstrating that early education intervention is effective in working with children with Down syndrome. Intervention services for children with Down syndrome are expanded by the Individuals with Disabilities Education Act (IDEA).

1990s Trisomic mice are created by genetic engineering to serve as a model for basic scientific research in Down syndrome.

2000   Scientists in Japan determine the genetic coding or base pair sequence for chromosome 21.

2001   The American Academy of Pediatrics Committee on Genetics publishes updated recommendations for pediatricians caring for children with Down syndrome.

2006–2007   Scientists publish three new and different approaches to prevention or amelioration of Down syndrome effects on the brain and cognition.

2007   The American College of Obstetricians and Gynecologists recommends that screening and invasive testing for Down syndrome and related chromosome abnormalities should be offered to all pregnant women.

ORGANIZATIONS TO CONTACT

The Arc of the United States
1010 Wayne Ave.
Suite 650
Silver Spring,
Maryland 20910
(301) 565-3842 /
(800) 433-5255
fax: (301) 565-3843 /
(301) 565-5342
info@thearc.org
www.thearc.org

The Arc of the United States advocates for the rights and full participation of all children and adults with intellectual and developmental disabilities. The organization works to improve systems of supports and services, connect families, inspire communities, and influence public policy. The Arc publishes several fact sheets and a state-specific family resource guide.

Association for Children with Down Syndrome (ACDS)
4 Fern Pl.
Plainview, NY 11803
(516) 933-4700
fax: (516) 933-9524
www.acds.org

ACDS is a New York–based association that offers educational, therapeutic, behavioral, and health-related services to persons with Down syndrome and their families. ACDS is dedicated to providing lifetime resources of exceptional quality, innovation, and inclusion for individuals with Down syndrome and other developmental disabilities and for their families.

Canadian Down Syndrome Society (CDSS)
811 Fourteenth St. NW
Calgary, Alberta,
Canada T2N 2A4
(403) 270-8500
fax: (403) 270-8291
dsinfo@cdss.ca
www.cdss.ca

CDSS is a national, nonprofit organization whose mission is to enhance the quality of life for all individuals who have Down syndrome. The CDSS accomplishes this mission by providing information and assistance to all those with an interest in Down syndrome, by advocating on behalf of individuals with Down syndrome in the areas of education, employment, and health care and by providing networking opportunities for parents and professionals in relevant fields.

Down Syndrome Information Alliance
925 L St., Suite 1200
Sacramento, CA 95814
(916) 658-1686
info@downsyndrome
info.org
www.downsyndrome
info.org

The Down Syndrome Information Alliance is an organization committed to providing resources, support, and education for families and professionals affected by Down syndrome so that individuals with Down syndrome may achieve their goals and lead fulfilling lives. The Down Syndrome Information Alliance publishes an online and print newsletter.

Down Syndrome International
Langdon Down
Centre 2A Langdon
Park
Teddington,
Middlesex TW11 9PS,
United Kingdom
444 845 230 0372
enquiries@down-
syndrome-int.org.
www.down-syndrome
-int.org/contacts/dsi-
contact

Down Syndrome International encourages research into the educational and developmental needs of individuals with Down syndrome. In order to meet this goal, the organization brings together parents, professionals, and international experts from around the world every three years to discuss current research, education, and advocacy programs at a world congress. Down Syndrome International has created an e-mail distribution list to promote international discussion and collaboration and serves as an information source for Down syndrome publications. Their publications include *Down Syndrome News and Update* (DSNU) and *Down Syndrome Research and Practice* (DSRP).

Down Syndrome Research Foundation & Resource Centre (DSRFR)
3580 Slocan St.
Vancouver, BC,
Canada V5M 3E8
(604) 431-9694
fax: (604) 431-9248
dsrf@sfu.ca
www.dsrf.org

DSRFR was formed in 1995 in response to the need, expressed by parents and professionals, for detailed and research-based information for themselves and for the community at large. The DSRFR has developed and collected numerous resources related to the medical issues, education, and development of individuals with Down syndrome.

International Mosaic Down Syndrome Association (IMDSA)
PO Box 1052
Franklin, TX 77856
(888) 637-5465
fax: (775) 295-9373
imdsapresident@
imdsa.com
www.imdsa.com

The IMDSA provides support information, and research to any family, individual, or professional whose life has been affected by mosaic Down syndrome. IMDSA provides support and information through its online support group, Web site, and quarterly newsletter.

National Association for Down Syndrome (NADS)
PO Box 206
Wilmette, IL 60091
(630) 325-9112
info@nads.org
www.nads.org

NADS is the oldest organization in the country serving individuals with Down syndrome and their families. NADS's mission is to ensure that all persons with Down syndrome have the opportunity to achieve their potential in all aspects of community life. The organization offers information, support, and advocacy. NADS publishes a bimonthly newsletter (*NADS News*) and several informational brochures about Down syndrome.

The National Down Syndrome Congress (NDSC)
1370 Center Dr., Suite 102
Atlanta, GA 30338
(770) 604-9500
fax: (770) 604-9898
info@ndsccenter.org
www.ndsccenter.org

The mission of the NDSC is to provide information, advocacy, and support concerning all aspects of life for individuals with Down syndrome. The organization strives to create a national climate in which all persons recognize and embrace the value and dignity of persons with Down syndrome and is committed to promoting the availability of and accessibility to a full range of opportunities and/or resources that meet individual and family needs. NDSC publishes *Down Syndrome* and has developed position papers and health-care guidelines.

National Down Syndrome Society (NDSS)
666 Broadway
New York, NY 10012
(800) 221-4602
fax: (212) 979-2873
info@ndss.org
www.ndss.org

The mission of the NDSS is to benefit people with Down syndrome and their families through national leadership in education, research, and advocacy. The organization increases public awareness and serves to discover underlying causes of Down syndrome through education, research, and advocacy. NDSS publishes a quarterly newsletter, *Update*, and a magazine for teens and young adults, *News & Views*. The society also offers brochures and a variety of books and videos.

FOR FURTHER READING

Books

William I. Cohen, Lynn Nadel, and Myra E. Madnick, eds., *Down Syndrome: Visions for the 21st Century.* New York: John Wiley and Sons, 2002.

Cliff Cunningham, *Down Syndrome: An Introduction for Parents.* Cornwall, UK: Souvenir, 2006.

Kellie Greenwald, *Kellie's Book: The Art of the Possible.* Windsor, CA: Rayve, 2008.

Jennifer Graf Groneberg, *Road Map to Holland: How I Found My Way Through My Son's First Two Years with Down Syndrome.* New York: Penguin, 2008.

Dennis McGuire and Brian Chicoine, *Mental Wellness in Adults with Down Syndrome: A Guide to Emotional and Behavioral Strengths and Challenges.* Bethesda, MD: Woodbine House, 2006.

Siegfried M. Pueschel, ed., *Adults with Down Syndrome.* Baltimore: Paul Brookes, 2006.

———, *A Parent's Guide to Down Syndrome: Toward a Brighter Future.* Rev. ed., Baltimore: Paul Brookes, 2001.

Mark Selikowitz, *Down Syndrome (The Facts).* Oxford: Oxford University Press, 2008.

Kathryn L. Soper, ed., *Gifts: Mothers Reflect on How Children with Down Syndrome Enrich Their Lives.* Bethesda, MD: Woodbine House, 2007.

Kate Strohm, *Siblings: Brothers and Sisters of Children with Special Needs.* Adelaide, South Australia: Wakefield, 2002.

Mitchell Zuckoff, *Choosing Naia: A Family's Journey.* Boston: Beacon, 2003.

Periodicals

American Academy of Pediatrics, "Health Supervision for Children with Down Syndrome," *Pediatrics*, vol. 107, no. 2, February 2001.

American College of Obstetricans and Gynecologists, "ACOG Practice Bulletin No. 88: Invasive Prenatal Testing for Aneuploidy," *Obstetrics & Gynecology*, vol. 100, no. 6, December 2007.

American College of Obstetricans and Gynecologists, "ACOG Practice Bulletin No. 77: Screening for Fetal Chromosomal Abnormalities," *Obstetrics & Gynecology*, vol. 109, no. 1, January 2007.

Patricia E. Bauer, "If the Test Says Down Syndrome," *Washington Post*, November 16, 2007.

Beverly Beckham, "Lucy's Learning. But Are Doctors?" *Boston Globe*, February 4, 2007.

Peter Birkenhead, "'Eugenics' or 'Freedom of Choice?'" Broadsheet, *Salon.com*, May 11, 2007.

Campbell K. Brasington, "What I Wish I Knew Then . . . Reflections from Personal Experiences in Counseling About Down Syndrome," *Journal of Genetic Counseling*, vol. 16, no. 6, 2007.

Tierney Fairchild and Greg Fairchild, "Rising to the Occasion: Reflections on Choosing Naia," *Leadership Perspectives in Developmental Disability*, vol. 3, no. 1, Spring 2003.

Jonathan Finer, "Study: Negativity Often Tied to Down Syndrome Diagnoses," *Washington Post*, April 29, 2005.

Amy Harmon, "Prenatal Test Puts Down Syndrome in Hard Focus," *New York Times*, May 9, 2007.

———, "The Problem with an Almost-Perfect Genetic World," *New York Times*, November 20, 2005.

Kathryn Jean Lopez, "Defining Life Down," *National Review*, November 30, 2005. www.nationalreview.com/lopez/lopez 200511300840.asp.

Linda Moran, "'Outing' My Kids," *Exceptional Parent*, March 2004.

Madeline Moran, "David!" *Exceptional Parent*, June 2003.

Julia Neuberger, "Should We Choose Our Children?" *Lancet*, April 15–April 21, 2006.

Roni Rabin, "Screen All Pregnancies for Down Syndrome, Doctors Say," *New York Times*, January 9, 2007.

Margaret Renkl, "Life with Anthony," *Parenting*, December/January, 2008.

Dave Reynolds, "Community Living Leads to Longer, Better Life for Those with Down Syndrome," *Inclusion Daily Express*, March 21, 2002.

Peter Schworm, "Down Syndrome: The Positives: Parents, Researcher Challenge Perceptions," *Boston Globe*, June 4, 2006.

B.G. Skotko and S.P. Levine, "What the Other Children Are Thinking: Brothers and Sisters of Persons with Down Syndrome," *American Journal of Medical Genetics*, vol. 142C, no. 3, 2006.

Rob Stein, "Down Syndrome Now Detectable in First Trimester: Earlier Diagnosis Allows More Time for Decisions," *Washington Post*, November 10, 2005.

M. Van Riper, "A Change of Plans: The Birth of a Child with Down Syndrome," *American Journal of Nursing*, vol. 103, 2003.

Claudia Wallis, "A Very Special Wedding," *Time*, July 16, 2006.

George F. Will, "Golly, What Did Jon Do?" *Newsweek*, January 29, 2007.

INDEX